FASTING

FORSAKING THE COMMON LEVELS OF CHRISTIANITY

LISA VAN VUUREN

DEDICATION

I dedicate this book to the Lord and His kingdom. Thank You, Lord, for being so ever-faithful in my life. Thank You for leading me to write this book. Thank You, Holy Spirit, for guiding me, quickening to me, and revealing to me. I could never have done this without You. I am humbled by the trust You have placed in me, and the patience that You have shown me.

Table of Contents

ACKNOWLEDGEMENTS

My deepest appreciation to Ruan, my wonderful, loving husband, and my two beautiful sons for supporting me in the writing of this book and affording me the time away from you to do so. I love you and treasure you more than you will ever know. Thank you also to all my close friends (you know who you are) for your love and support.

INTRODUCTION

I have known that this book was coming for a long time. Patiently I waited on the Lord to birth this book in my spirit. I am tremendously humbled that the Lord chose to write a book on the subject of fasting through me. The first Christian book that I read after being born-again was Derek Prince's *How to Fast Successfully*. I believe that it helped shape me into the believer that I am today.
During the time that I read Derek Prince's book on fasting, the other believers in my very small circle of born-again friends tried to dissuade me to fast. However, I read his book and I felt an excitement grow within me. I was unstoppable. I began fasting just as Derek Prince indicated in his book, and I was never the same again. Six years later, in 2012, I began a fasting ministry and now, nine years later, I can honestly say that fasting has been a very important part of my walk with God.

In this book I (humbly) hope to do what Derek Prince did so many years ago for me. I hope to educate believers about fasting, how it works, the tremendous power it releases, and all the different types of fasting as the Lord has revealed it to me.
As you read this book, may the Lord open your eyes to the truth, and stir up a fire in you to forsake the common levels of Christianity. I honestly believe that this is a book written for this space in time. We are moving into the end times, and we can no longer be luke-warm. As believers we have to rise up and move in God's power. May this book be the catalyst that gets you there.

Lisa van Vuuren
Prophetess and Teacher

Founder and overseer of *Daniel Ministries: Freeing the Nations from Captivity through Prayer and Fasting.*

<u>PRAYER</u>

Heavenly Father, I pray that every believer reading this book will find what they need to equip them as great prayer warriors for Your kingdom. May we rise up as Your great end-time army, equipped and ready for battle. Lord, give each person reading this book a personal revelation of the contents so that they can make these strategies their own, in Jesus' name. Amen.

CHAPTER 1

FASTING?

"Then I proclaimed a fast there at the river Ahava, that we might humble ourselves before our God, <u>to seek from Him the right way for us</u> and our little ones and all our possessions." Ezra 8:21 (NKJV)

You may have wondered about the name of the chapter. Let me tell you where it came from. That is exactly the question everyone would ask me when they learned that I was in the habit of fasting. They would give me a puzzled look and say, "Fasting?" And I am not talking about unbelievers. Years ago in 2006 when I began to fast it was not something that was widely practiced in Christian circles. In fact, as word got around, groups of believers would approach me and ask if I could teach them about fasting. Even pastors would ask me to say something about fasting when we had camps or prayer meetings.

I loved teaching people about fasting. It was my passion. I had realized from experience how incredibly powerful fasting can be. I witnessed it first hand in my own life, and I wanted to place every believer on that same powerful journey. I experienced accelerated spiritual growth, saw amazing answers to my prayers, and I had a very vivid sense of the Lord leading me on a specific path – literally directing my every step.

I realized from the start that this is how it is when you serve God: He leads you on a specific path – a path that He has personally set out for you.

"You saw me before I was born. Every day of my life was recorded in Your book. Every moment was laid out before a single day had passed." Psalm 139:16 (NLT)

I believe that is where many believers miss the plot. We tend to think that when we are born-again 'it is done', when actually 'it has only begun'. So many believers are aimless believers – not really going anywhere or working towards anything, when God really has a *specific* path for us. These aimless believers will tell you that the only thing you need to do is to love God. This is most certainly true. Loving God is the foundation of what we believe in as Christ's ones, however, I have realized that serving God is not nearly that simple. Let's look at it from a parent's point of view. Every parent loves their children, and has specific expectations for them. It is not merely enough that your child loves you back. For example, you also expect your child to go to school and get good grades. You want your child to choose good friends and not to fall into bad habits. Surely, you also want your child to be obedient when you discipline him. These are only examples of expectations you may have for your child.

Well, it is the same with God the Father. He loves that we love Him, but He also wants to teach us spiritual principles, He wants us to draw near to Him and have an intimate relationship with Him, He wants us to dine on a steady diet of the Word, He wants us to walk in the plans that He has for us, and He wants all these things to flow forth from *the fact that we love Him*. We do not do these things to *earn* His love, but we do them *because* we love Him.

"Little children, let us not love [merely] in theory or in speech but in deed and in truth (in practice and in sincerity)." I John 3:18 (AMPC)

Now here is the thing: If the Lord has set out a specific path for each of us, then He expects us to walk in it, and walking on that path is most definitely not effortless. From our side we must make a continuous, concerted effort to *stay on that path*. It could certainly happen that we become distracted and wonder from the path, or take a wrong fork in the path by making the wrong decision.

"Enter through the narrow gate. For wide is the gate and <u>broad is the road that leads to destruction</u>, and many enter through it. But small is the gate and <u>narrow the road that leads to life, and only a few find it</u>." Matthew 7:13-14 (NIV)

When we are born-again, we have essentially 'found the road to life' as this Scripture indicates. However, *finding* the road is not enough. We must also *travel* this road to reach its destination, which is 'life'. To *stay* on the narrow road that leads to life and to *steadily progress* on it, you will have to continue with caution and much prayer. You will not be able to smile and love your way through it. You will need guidance from the Lord, because your own thoughts and understanding (should you lean on them), may cause you to inadvertently stray from the path.

"Trust in the Lord with all your heart, And lean not on your own understanding; <u>in all your ways acknowledge Him, And He shall direct your paths</u>." Proverbs 3:5-6 (NKJV)

It seems to me that the Lord has a specific path for each one of us, and if you are not consciously trying to walk in it, then you may very well stray from it. It also seems that you may need all the help you can get to walk (and keep on walking) on that path. Isn't that why the Word says:

"Your word is a lamp to my feet and a light to my path." Psalm 119:105 (AMPC)

Clearly, staying on the path that God has for you is not easy. Let us be honest, you need the Lord's help. Now here is the good part. Did you know that the Lord could teach you what to choose to stay on His path?

"Who is the man who reverently fears and worships the Lord? <u>Him shall He teach in the way that he should choose.</u>" Psalm 25:12 (AMPC)

That is what happens when you fast regularly: God begins to lead you and guide you in amazing ways – making sure that you stay on that path that He has for you. He literally teaches you the way in which you should make your choices in order to stay on His path.

"Wait for and expect the Lord <u>and keep and heed His way, and He will exalt you to inherit the land.</u>" Psalm 37:34 (AMPC)

<u>So, what is fasting and how do we fast?</u>

Firstly, I want to make it clear that I am certainly not 'all knowing' on the topic of fasting. I also do not have theological degrees. What I do possess, however, is experience and an intimate walk with God. This book is being written by me in obedience to God's instruction. Therefore I believe that the Lord wants me to share the things that I have learned from Him in this book.

I have learned that fasting is merely a sacrifice that we make in order to release more spiritual power as we pray and seek the Lord. We give up something that is of great value to us e.g. food is a basic necessity for all human beings. We need food in order to survive. When we fast and sacrifice food, we are saying to the Lord, *'Lord, I know I need food to survive, but for this period of time I am sacrificing that basic need to show You that my need for You is greater.'*

We can fast in many different ways. Fasting from food is merely one example. I have learned that I can fast from anything that is important to me – not only food. I can also fast from things that I find difficult to abstain from. When you fast, you must make a decision before each fast about exactly what it is that you will be abstaining from – you must set the perimeters of your fast *before* you begin.

Let me give you an example: When you fast, you may fast from food. Alternatively, you can eat food, and fast from all liquids, or you can fast from both food and liquids. In any fast where you abstain from liquids altogether I advise that your fast does not exceed more than three days for health reasons. Also, when you fast from food, make sure that you hydrate properly throughout the day. I have done a forty day fast from food, and when you do a long fast like that from food I recommend the following:

- Make sure to drink lots of fluids throughout the day.
- Try to take in drinking fibre every day. Tony Ferguson has a product called Dietary Fibre that you can mix with water and drink in a glass. This will keep you from becoming constipated, and keep your gut going.
- Take your fast day by day. When I fasted I made a conscious effort not to look at the big picture e.g. I stil have 39 days of fasting left. No, each morning I got up, I would say to myself: *'Okay, I am fasting today, I just need to get through today.'*
- Don't take on too many prayer points when you do such a long fast. Prioritize and take only the most important points that you know you will be able to cover in prayer *every day* – remember, your fast is only as powerful as your prayer!
- You will need lots of gum for your breath, as the lack of food tends to bring about a bad breath.
- Resist the temptation to tell people you are fasting. Surely, with such a long fast you want every reward that you can get. Don't give away your rewards by bragging about your fast.
- When I undertook this fast I was at home for five months on maternity leave. This gave me plenty of time to pray and when I felt weak, I was in the safety of my home. If you are a working person, make sure your work schedule will allow such a prolonged fast.

- When you have finished your fast, you must be very careful to introduce solid foods to your gut very slowly. Going from no food to solids overnight can be very painful and unhealthy. Eat soft foods for the first week or two after which you can slowly incorporate solid food into your diet. It will take patience if you don't want to harm your gut.

You can also abstain from eating only specific types of foods in your fast. You may fast from all social media and television – even your phone. Years ago, I learned about a 'word fast'. In a 'word fast' you fast (therefore refrain) from speaking any negative words e.g. complaints, gossiping, negativity, anger-venting, etc. Recently, a close friend of mine told me about a fast that she was doing on negative and destructive thoughts e.g. thoughts of condemnation, thoughts of not being good enough, thoughts of rejection, etc. Each day she had to fast from a specific thought, and with it she had to renounce that evil thought out loud (renounce meaning to refuse to follow, refuse to obey any further) and confirm the opposite of that thought out loud throughout the day. This seems very powerful, especially if one should struggle with specific, negative thoughts. You could, for instance, do a twenty-one day fast on thoughts of rejection, if you find that you struggle in that specific area. That would be especially difficult if you have recurring thoughts of rejection. Some time ago I was engaged in an immense battle against addiction. Addiction is very prominent in my bloodline. As I was praying one day the Lord instructed me to fast specifically from my addiction (which was television). He showed me that if I fast for deliverance from an addiction, that I should fast from that specific addiction in order to starve the bad habit.

In my years of fasting I have learned that one of the most difficult areas to surrender to the Lord is your time. It is easy to do "Christian things" that you like to spend your time doing, but when it comes to giving your time to do exclusively that which the Lord wants you to do, it becomes a whole different ball game. That makes for a powerful fast. You may spend your time doing what you need to do, but when it comes to your time to relax, you may not choose what you wish to do. Instead you have to pray, worship, or do Bible study. It sounds easy enough, but believe me, your flesh will be screaming for release after two days.

One of the most important reasons for you to fast, is to repair your relationship with the Lord. Fasting removes interferences in the communication between you and God. It serves to focus your attention on God alone by removing those things that may distract you e.g. food, television, addictions, etc. Removing distractions is a sacrifice when you remove those things that take up your attention. The things that distract you and take up your time are usually things that you deem important and that you take pleasure in doing. When you fast from them you are able to focus all your attention on the Lord alone. In addition, you can use the time that you would have spent on the distraction to draw closer to God in prayer. It is then also appropriate to repent for those things that distract from your relationship and intimacy with the Lord.

"Therefore also now, says the Lord, turn and keep on coming to Me with all your heart, with fasting, with weeping, and with mourning [until every hindrance is removed and the broken fellowship is restored]." Joel 2:12 (AMPC)

The Bible also reveals to us that we are able to fast from sleep:

"But we commend ourselves in every way as [true] servants of God: through great endurance, in tribulation and suffering, in hardships and privations, in sore straits and calamities, in beatings, imprisonments, riots, labors, sleepless watching, hunger" II Corinthians 6:4-5 (AMPC)

Abstaining from sleep is a very effective way of fasting. Like food, sleep is also a basic human need. When you fast from sleep you are saying to the Lord, *'Yes Lord, I need sleep to survive, but I choose You over that need.'* In addition you are able to put in much more prayer time as you pray throughout the night. When you fast from sleep you do not have to stay up for the entire night. Remember: you set out your own fasting perimeters (with the guidance of the Lord, of course). You may, for instance, decide that your fast will consist of depriving yourself from sleep from 24:00 to 02:00 every morning, which you then spend in prayer and worship and reading of the Word.

When you fast and give up something that is really important to you, you are fulfilling the Scripture that says:

"If anyone desires to come after Me, let him deny himself, and take up his cross, and follow Me. For whoever desires to save his life will lose it, but whoever loses his life for My sake will find it." Matthew 16:24-25 (NKJV)

So you can see that there are many different things that we can fast from. Of course, I would advise you to be led by the Spirit in what you choose to fast from.

Did you know that God is the Creator of fasting? God alone is a Creator. In the Book of Exodus God calls Moses to the mountain where Moses fasts for 40 days and 40 nights without food or water.

"So he was there with the LORD forty days and forty nights; he neither ate bread nor drank water." Exodus 34:28 (NKJV)

Whilst there, the Lord gave Moses the Law for the Israelites. Among these are many different fasts that the Lord wanted the Israelites to practice throughout each year.

Clearly, the Lord expects from His people to serve Him with fasting. Yes, you read it correctly. I said, '*serve* Him with fasting'. Part of being a *servant* to the Lord is to serve Him with fasting and prayers. This is Biblical and New Testament.

"Now there was one, Anna, a prophetess, the daughter of Phanuel, of the tribe of Asher. She was of a great age, and had lived with a husband seven years from her virginity; and this woman was a widow of about eighty-four years, who did not depart from the temple, <u>but served God with fastings and prayers night and day</u>." Luke 2:36-37 (NKJV)

Fasting is also a way of consecrating yourself for God. To consecrate yourself means that you wholly dedicate yourself to something (or someone) of great importance. It is the act of setting yourself apart and completely dedicating yourself to the Lord.

"Now on the twenty-fourth day of this month, the Israelites were assembled with fasting and in sackcloth and with earth upon their heads. And the Israelites separated themselves from all foreigners and stood and confessed their sins and the iniquities of their fathers. And they stood in their place and read from the Book of the Law of the Lord their God for a fourth of the day, and for another fourth of it they confessed and worshiped the Lord their God." Nehemiah 9:1-3 (AMPC)

Look carefully at this Scripture and you will see that the Israelites called a fast and consecrated themselves by setting them apart from all foreigners. As they separated themselves they spent their time seeking and worshiping the Lord and reading from His Word. When we enter into a fast, it is important that we, too, set ourselves apart from the world. In this day and age where everyone has a career it can be difficult, but the main idea is that you make a specific time within your fast where you separate yourself from others in order to seek the Lord in prayer.

"But when you pray, go into your [most] private room, and, closing the door, pray to your Father, Who is in secret; and your Father, Who sees in secret, will reward you in the open."
Matthew 6:6 (AMPC)

Although I myself am a working woman and face challenges with time between my ministry, my family, work, cooking etc. I try to make a point in each fast to have a little time to myself so that I can seek the Lord in prayer. Of course, at work I pray throughout the day – the intimate type of prayer that you share with the Lord in your thoughts. However, I still try to separate myself from all the buzz so that I am able to just focus on the Lord alone without any interferences or disruptions.

If you decide to go the route of fasting, then my advice to you would be to cultivate good fasting habits from the start. Let us take a look at a few of those good habits:

<u>Good Fasting Habits:</u>

Firstly, when you fast it is always good to keep a fasting journal. In your journal, you can write the date of each fast, how long you are fasting for, as well as a list of the things you are fasting about. You can fast about more than one issue at a time, however, I would advise you to refrain from taking on too many fasting directives in any one fast. You may find that you are not able to cover each fasting directive thoroughly in prayer, and feel overwhelmed. Instead, try to fast more often with fewer fasting directives. That will give you the opportunity to cover more fasting directives, whilst also soaking them properly in much prayer. You must have specific points that you are fasting about. Do not fast in general. Be specific about the reasons for your fast and note them clearly in your journal. I find it very encouraging each time I go back into my fasting journal when God answers my prayers.

In such a case, I write the date that the Lord answered my prayer next to the specific entry I made when I was fasting about that particular point. It is sure to motivate you when you page back in your fasting journal and you see all the answers to your prayers. In fact, many times you will find that the Lord has answered prayers of which you had forgotten that you had prayed them in the first place. Now when you decide which points you will be fasting about, be sure to acknowledge the Lord.

"...<u>in all your ways acknowledge Him</u>, And He shall direct your paths." Proverbs 3:6 (NKJV)

I have developed a habit before each fast of asking the Lord whether there is something *He* wants me to include in my fast. This has helped me tremendously in the past. Many years ago (when I was still new on the concept of fasting), I did the same. On the morning that my fast began, I asked the Lord to show me if there was something that He wanted me to include in my fast. To be honest, I really didn't expect an answer. However, that morning I felt a strong leading that the Lord wanted me to fast about my son's after-school care facility. My son was in Grade 2 at the time. I didn't really understand why I had to fast about the after-school care facility. I felt that it was adequate as it was, but I wanted to be faithful with what I felt the Lord was giving me, so I obeyed. I finished my fast successfully that day, and never gave it another thought, until three months later. I was at work one day when I had a call from the owner of the after-school care facility that my son was attending. She had called to let me know that they were permanently closing the facility that same day, and that I needed to make different arrangements for my son from that point on. Well, I was truly shaken up. I was a full-time working mother, and the call came in the middle of the month.

I had no idea what to do. As I sat pondering my situation, the Holy Spirit brought to my remembrance the fast that I had done about my son's after-school care facility. I quickly paged back in my fasting journal, and I saw that three months earlier the Lord had led me to pray for the situation that I found myself in. A peace came over me as I realized that God knew this was coming, and that He had already prepared everything for me. I drove around that afternoon searching for a facility for my son, when his class teacher called me. I had briefly spoken to her when I picked my son up from school, so she was aware of my situation. She called to tell me about a great after-school care facility run by remedial teachers who had a passion for children and only accepted new children on referral. She had referred me to them, and they were already waiting for me. Many years later, when my son was about nineteen years old, he told me how that the first after-school care facility had a very negative effect on him as a child. He was a very quiet, emotional child, and they had disciplined him harshly when he had mostly been innocent. Being the quiet child that he was, he never told anyone. He merely kept quiet and endured it. But God knew what was happening to my child, and on that day when I asked Him if there was something He wanted me to pray about, He addressed a serious issue in my child's life that I was not even aware of at the time.

In all the years that I have been fasting I have also learned that, when the Lord gives me revelation about something important, it is because He wants me to fast about it. My most powerful fasts have come from when I am obedient and place God's guidance ahead of my own needs. I realized the importance of this when I was sitting in my bath a few years ago. I was deeply engrossed in prayer when the Lord suddenly broke through and began to speak to me.

It turns out I was fasting at the time, and whilst praying the Lord spoke clearly into my spirit and said, *'Why is it that when I speak to you directly about something, that you don't deem it important enough to include it in your fast? Look at My servant Daniel for an example. Although it was written in the Scriptures that I would deliver the Israelites from captivity after 70 years, even then Daniel knelt down and fasted and prayed about it.'*

"in the first year of his reign I, Daniel, understood by the books the number of the years specified by the word of the LORD through Jeremiah the prophet, that He would accomplish seventy years in the desolations of Jerusalem. Then I set my face toward the Lord God to make request by prayer and supplications, with fasting, sackcloth, and ashes."
Daniel 9:2-3 (NKJV)

Daniel became my example. I began to fast about the promises that God made to me, and the revelations He had given me. Daniel knew that this promise from the Lord was written in the Scriptures, yet he still took it upon himself to pray and seek the Lord for the Israelite's deliverance – reminding the Lord of His promise in the Scriptures.

One morning a few years back I was driving to work on a fasting day. As usual I was praying in the car on my way. I was seeking the Lord, asking Him if there was anything He wanted me to include in my fast. Unexpectedly, the Holy Spirit whispered into my ear, *'Pray and ask Me to teach you the songs and shouts of deliverance.'*

"You are a hiding place for me; You , Lord, preserve me from trouble, <u>You surround me with songs and shouts of deliverance</u>." *Psalms 32:7 (AMPC)*

You can see that seeking the Lord, when it comes to your fasting directives, is especially powerful. If you acknowledge God when you draw up your prayer points for your fast, He will come through for you when you least expect it, and prepare you for things to come – directing your path.

When you want to undertake a fast, it is always good to decide on the duration of the fast beforehand. Determine how long you want your fast to be (depending on how desperate you are for God's intervention), and try, as far as possible, to always stick to your resolution. There have been times when I have undertaken a fast without setting out a specific period. That is usually when I have reached a breaking point about some issue in my life. In such a case, I would speak to the Lord and commit to fasting until that situation is resolved. I would speak to the Lord throughout the fast and say something like, *'Lord, I am going to fast until this situation breaks. Either it breaks, or I will break – please let it not be me. See how desperate I am for Your intervention and deliverance!'* When there is a very serious issue in your life (maybe something that you need deliverance from) I would suggest that you start off by doing a series of short fasts about the issue. If there is no change, you may think about doing a prolonged fast e.g. seven days, ten days, twenty-one days, and even thirty or forty days. If after a prolonged fast you are still desperate, then I would suggest the type of fast where you decide to keep fasting until that situation in your life breaks. I had a lady who worked with me some years back. We sat together in the same office day in, and day out, and eventually (being in such constant, close proximity to each other) she realized that I practiced fasting. She had many questions, and told me that she wanted to fast for her daughter who was unable to get a job. She desperately wanted to do a food fast, but she admitted that it felt completely impossible for her to fast from food. She loved food and couldn't endure fasting from it. Eventually, desperate as she was, she decided to fast from food for two hours a day. As she was able to achieve this, she moved on to three hours a day. She gradually increased the time duration of her fast until she was able to go without food for twenty-four hours at a time. A few months later, she came to me with her testimony. She had been fasting and praying for her daughter to get a job, and her daughter was blessed with a fantastic job and great benefits to go with it. She felt overwhelmed by the goodness of the Lord.

An important Biblical principle to remember when you fast, is that fasting is an intimate thing between you and the Lord. Get into the habit, right from the start, of keeping your fast a secret between you and the Lord.

"And when you fast, don't make it obvious, as the hypocrites do, for they try to look miserable and dishevelled so people will admire them for their fasting. I tell you the truth, that is the only reward they will ever get. But when you fast, comb your hair and wash your face. Then no one will notice that you are fasting, except your Father, who knows what you do in private. And your Father, who sees everything, will reward you." Matthew 6:16-18 (NLT)

When you fast (and you are serious about it) there can be no bragging, no looking for human admiration, and no looking for 'sympathy' from people because of how 'difficult' your fast is. If you are serious about your fast, you will keep it quiet. If you live with family members it may be evident to them when you fast. You may share with them, but be very careful how you share, and always check your motives in your heart before you do. Do not share with them to earn their admiration, but only the necessary information that is needed for their understanding of your situation, if necessary. After a fast you may share your testimonies with others.

"And they have defeated him by the blood of the Lamb <u>and by their testimony</u>." Revelation 12:11 (NLT)

Even then, I advise you to check your motives in your heart. Do not share a testimony if your motive is to gain admiration. Share only if your motive is to give God all the glory for what He has done for you. This way you will also be able to introduce others to the powerful way of fasting.

CHAPTER 2

FASTING FROM THE HEART

"As in water face reflects face, So a man's heart reveals the man."
Proverbs 27:19 (NKJV)

In Chapter 1 I mentioned one of the most important reasons for fasting, which is to repair the relationship between you and the Lord. This may seem somewhat puzzling to you, as you may feel that your relationship with the Lord is not broken. On the contrary, the spiritual breach that occurred on the day that Adam ate the forbidden fruit caused sin to enter in to the world, and this unfortunately affects all of us. When you were born, you were born in iniquity (sin). King David had a very clear revelation of this. He was conscious of the fact the he was born in iniquity and that he was a sinner.

"Have mercy upon me, O God, according to Your steadfast love; according to the multitude of Your tender mercy and loving-kindness blot out my transgressions. Wash me thoroughly [and repeatedly] from my iniquity and guilt and cleanse me and make me wholly pure from my sin! For I am conscious of my transgressions and I acknowledge them; my sin is ever before me. Against You, You only, have I sinned and done that which is evil in Your sight, so that You are justified in Your sentence and faultless in Your judgment. Behold I was brought forth in [a state of] iniquity; my mother was sinful who conceived me [and I too am sinful]." Psalm 51:1-5 (AMPC)

Every person is born in sin and a sinner, we inherited this from Adam. Furthermore, no person is without sin.

"If we say that we have no sin, we deceive ourselves, and the truth is not in us. If we confess our sins, He is faithful and just to forgive us our sins and to cleanse us from all unrighteousness. If we say that we have not sinned, we make Him a liar, and His word is not in us." I John 1:8-10 (NKJV)

You may be free from sins such as murder, adultery, or theft, but it is also a sin to carry resentment in your heart, or to have the wrong motives for doing something. When you are born-again the Lord will firstly bring to your attention the more obvious sin that you need to deal with in your life. But as you draw closer to the Lord, He may begin to go deeper and deeper into your heart and mind – revealing to you those sins that are mostly hidden from you. These are the 'not so obvious' sins, and are mostly also the most difficult to deal with. This means that there is sin that stands between you and the Lord, causing a breach. As the Lord reveals these sins to you and you remove them, you draw closer and closer to the Lord, thereby repairing the breach (relationship) between you and Him.

"<u>Draw near to God and He will draw near to you.</u> Cleanse your hands, you sinners; and purify your hearts, you double-minded." James 4:8 (NKJV)

This Scripture reveals to you the way to draw nearer to God, which is to cleanse your hands, and purify your heart. The closer you draw to the Lord and the deeper you go into His presence, the more conscious you will become of your sinful nature as He reveals to you those things that stand between you and Him. I have seen this in my own walk with the Lord. Every time that the Lord reveals something to me that stands between us, I make it a priority to fast and pray about it until something breaks. The more I do this, the greater the intimacy between me and the Lord becomes. I don't use the word 'intimacy' lightly. Intimacy speaks of a closeness between two people that are in a relationship.

Intimacy cannot be reached overnight – it takes time. It takes trust to be built up between two faithful and committed people in a relationship. Both have to show that they care, listen to each other, and be faithful as they are entrusted with the other's secrets. There are levels of intimacy in any relationship. Through fasting I have experienced the deeper levels of intimacy with the Lord. I have found that my relationship with the Lord has become so real, that it feels more real to me than anything on this earth that I physically experience. I have developed a trust in Him that I find difficult to explain to others. I find that when the Lord speaks to me clearly, it overrides anything that anyone on this earth can say to me. Through personal experience I have learned to act on every word that He says, and every revelation He gives. It is an emotional and spiritual closeness that cannot be equalled. This type of intimacy with the Lord is available to every believer. All you need to do is practice James 4:8 – draw nearer to God by cleansing your hands and purifying your heart.

"Blessed (happy, enviably fortunate, and spiritually prosperous – possessing the happiness produced by the experience of God's favour and especially conditioned by the revelation of His grace, regardless of their outward conditions) are the pure in heart, for they shall see God!" Matthew 5:8 (AMPC)

The heart and fasting are very closely connected. In fact, I would even say that fasting is very much a heart-thing. When you fast, you cry out to the Lord. But your cries will not be heard if your heart is not right before the Lord, and if you do not fast with the right motives in your heart.

"The Lord said to me, Do not pray for this people for their good. Though they fast, I will not hear their cry; and though they offer burnt offering and cereal offering [without heartfelt surrender to Me, or by offering it too late], I will not accept them." Jeremiah 14:11-12 (AMPC)

Understand one important fact in your walk as a born-again believer: *God always looks at the heart. Everything* in life springs forth from your heart.

"Keep and guard your heart with all vigilance and above all that you guard, <u>for out of it flow the springs of life.</u>" Proverbs 4:23 (AMPC)

In Chapter 1 we spoke about the good habits that you need to cultivate as you make fasting a way of life. Another good habit that you should pursue, is to *always check your heart before* you undertake a fast.

"So if you are presenting your offering at the altar, and while there you remember that your brother has something [such as a grievance or legitimate complaint] against you, leave your offering there at the altar and go. First make peace with your brother, and then come and present your offering." Matthew 5:23-24 (AMP)

I have personally experienced the truth of this Scripture in my life. About a year ago the Lord began to show me that there was something that I needed to do for Him. He made me aware of the fact that my time to perform this task was running out. Wanting desperately to be obedient and feeling pressed for time I fasted and prayed, but for the first time in my life I didn't get any guidance from the Lord as to what I should be doing. The Lord only kept on showing me that time was running out, and I was late. I continued doing what I knew best to do: I fasted and prayed and I kept crying out to the Lord to show me what I needed to do for Him. One Sunday I was especially desperate. I remember worshiping the whole morning in my prayer room until well after noon. Yet, it felt as if there was an impenetrable wall between me and the Lord, and no matter what I did, I couldn't break through. Very discouraged, and heartbroken that I was unable to hear from the Lord, I crawled into my bed that afternoon.

I was emotionally drained, and tearfully I told the Lord that my heart is broken, because I could not hear from Him. For the first time in our relationship I felt blocked out, and I didn't take it well at all. I fell asleep on my bed that afternoon, tears still wet on my cheeks. As I slept the Lord spoke very clearly to me in a dream. He showed me that a friend of mine (also a believer) had taken an offense when I had spoken to her about sexual sin in her life, and this offense was standing between me and the Lord – interfering with our communication and our intimacy. I realized that I needed to sort out the offense very quickly so that I could hear from the Lord again. Now I want you to understand, when I spoke to my friend about the sin in her life, that I did so in love. The fact of the matter was not that I had done something wrong, but that she had taken an offense. My point is that, regardless of the fact whether you are wrong or right: if the Lord brings something like this to your attention you must immediately humble yourself and try to make amends.

"Blessed (enjoying enviable happiness, spiritually prosperous – with life-joy and satisfaction in God's favour and salvation, regardless of their outward conditions) are the makers and maintainers of peace, for they shall be called the sons of God!" Matthew 5:9 (AMPC)

I approached my friend, humbled myself (no matter if I had spoken the truth from the Word), and apologised if I had in any way hurt her feelings, or made her feel rejected. Understand that I did not apologise for *what* I said – I can never apologise and make excuses for the truth in God's Word. I apologised for the fact that I might have carried it over in a way that hurt her. I may apologise for my own behaviour for I am human and most definitely make mistakes, but I will never apologise for, or render insignificant the Word and truth of God in order to spare someone's feelings. If any mistake was made, it was from my side. God's Word is perfect.

"As for God, His way is perfect! The word of the Lord is tested and tried..." Psalm 18:30 (AMPC)

When I apologised to my friend, my apology was truly from my heart. Yes, I wanted to hear the Lord's voice again, but I also did not want her to harbour an offense against me. I wanted to impact her life positively for God's kingdom. I realized as a child of God, even though she was committing wilful sin, He still loved her, and I had a much better chance to impact her life for His kingdom if we were at a good place with each other.

Without realizing it at the time, the Lord was taking me through a much needed learning curve regarding Matthew 5:23-24. After apologising to my friend, the Lord showed me two more people that had taken an offense against me. Even though I felt that I did not do anything wrong, I humbled myself and apologised from my heart, because I realized again that God is a peoples-God. He is in the people-business. People are important to Him, and being one of His representatives here on earth, I had to make sure that God is always portrayed as a God of love through my own behaviour.

Going back to the start of my story where I was fasting and crying out to God, I need you to understand one very important fact. Fasting and prayer gets God's attention. When we pray and fast God turns to us, and the only thing that He looks at when He turns to us, is our hearts. As we look at the faces of people that we engage with, so God looks at the heart when we engage Him in prayer and fasting.

"But the LORD said to Samuel, 'Do not look at his appearance or at his physical stature, because I have refused him. <u>For the LORD does not see as man sees; for man looks at the outward appearance, but the LORD looks at the heart.</u>'" I Samuel 16:7 (NKJV)

There is something that you need to understand about your heart. The heart is the place in your being where you store up valuable things – things that you treasure, and things that are of value to you.

"A good man out of the good treasure of his heart brings forth good things, and an evil man out of the evil treasure brings forth evil things." Matthew 12:35 (NKJV)

If you think of your being in terms of your house, your safe would be your heart. In your home your safe would be the place where you store your most valuable items – expensive items that you hold dear. It is the same with your heart. Your heart is the place within your being in which you store things that you cherish and love most. That is why Scripture says:

"For where your treasure is, there will your heart be also." Matthew 6:21 (AMPC)

The heart is connected to treasure – to all the things that you treasure. Now at home you are able to open your safe at any time in order to look through its contents. It is not so with your heart.

"The heart is deceitful above all things, and it is exceedingly perverse and corrupt and severely, mortally sick! Who can know it [perceive, understand, be acquainted with his own heart and mind]? I the Lord search the mind, I try the heart..." Jeremiah 17:9-10 (AMPC)

The treasure in your heart (whether good treasure, or evil treasure) is hidden from you by your heart. You have no way of inspecting what is inside your heart. The only way of knowing what is inside your heart is to ask the Holy Spirit to search your heart for you.

"For the Spirit searches all things, yes, the deep things of God." I Corinthians 2:10 (NKJV)

Only the Holy Spirit is able to access your heart where you store your treasure, and only He can reveal to you what is contained within it.

Matthew 12:35 reveals to us that there are two types of treasures hidden in your heart: Evil treasure, and good treasure. As servants of God we have to make sure that our hearts are clean by removing the evil treasure from it.

"Search me [thoroughly], O God, and know my heart! Try me and know my thoughts! And see if there is any wicked or hurtful way in me, and lead me in the way everlasting."
Psalm 139:23-24 (AMPC)

That being said, I do not believe there is one person on this earth with a perfect heart, but I do believe that the Lord expects us to be in a continual process of cleansing. Hence, the good habit of asking the Lord to search your heart before each fast. This enables you to repent for sins and forgive any people that you have taken an offense with. Then, when you cry out to the Lord in fasting and prayer and He turns to you and looks at your heart, your prayers will be heard on high. Now I want you to be aware that, when you begin to make it a habit to ask the Lord to search your heart, that He will not only show you the 'superficial' sins that you can quickly rectify. After some time of searching your heart, the Lord may begin to reveal deeper, more difficult issues you struggle with that are all hidden in your heart. These may not be so easily dealt with. It may take patience, and much fasting and prayer from your side to address these issues. I have learned that the deeper the Lord goes into my heart, the more difficult it is for me to deal with the evil treasures that He reveals to me. When you ask the Lord to search your heart before each fast, get into the habit of repenting for that which the Lord shows you *before* and *during* your fast.

When you ask the Holy Spirit to search your heart before your fast, ask Him also to search if your motives in your heart are true. Then, when you undertake your fast, you are sure that you are not doing it for all the wrong reasons e.g. weight loss. Never undertake a fast when your motive is to lose weight in the process.

Your goal must not be weight loss, but to *"set yourself [determinedly, as your vital need] to seek the Lord"* II *Chronicles 20:3 (AMPC)* for those spiritual needs that you have listed. God does not react to a diet, but to heartfelt fasting and prayer from a pure heart. When you fast, your fast must indicate the condition of your heart. A humble, repentant heart bowed before God in heartfelt surrender, will always get God's attention and cause your prayers to be heard.

A humble heart is very important to the Lord. Fasting is a way of humbling yourself before God, because fasting is also the time when we must come before the Lord in repentance for our sins.

"Then I proclaimed a fast there, at the river Ahava, <u>that we might humble ourselves before our God</u>..." Ezra 8:21 (AMPC)

Humble means to feel modest and undeserving. To humble yourself is to do or say something to show that you know you have been wrong, or that you have behaved with too much pride. When you humble yourself before God through fasting, you are in effect saying to God, *'Lord, I ask for Your help. I know I am not deserving, but without You I cannot.'* Take a look at this Biblical example of the tax collector and you will see exactly what it means to humble yourself.

"Two men went up into the temple [enclosure] to pray, the one a Pharisee and the other a tax collector. The Pharisee took his stand ostentatiously and began to pray thus before and with himself: God, I thank You that I am not like the rest of men- extortioners (robbers), swindlers [unrighteous in heart and life], adulterers- or even like this tax collector here. I fast twice a week; give tithes of all that I gain. But the tax collector, [merely] standing at a distance, would not even lift up his eyes to heaven, but kept striking his breast, saying, O God, be favourable (be gracious, be merciful) to me, the especially wicked sinner that I am! I tell you, this man went down to his home justified (forgiven and made upright and in right standing with God), rather than the other man" Luke 18:10-13 (AMPC)

There is a very important Biblical principle to remember when fasting and humbling yourself:

"...for everyone who exalts himself will be humbled, but <u>he who humbles himself will be exalted</u>." Luke 18:14 (AMPC)

When we humble ourselves before God in fasting it opens God's heart to us:

"When Ahab heard these words of Elijah, he tore his clothes, put sackcloth on his flesh, fasted, lay in sackcloth, and went quietly. And the word of the Lord came to Elijah the Tishbite, saying, Do you see how Ahab humbles himself before Me? Because he humbles himself before Me, I will not bring the evil in his lifetime, but in his son's day I will bring the evil upon his house." I Kings 21:27-29 (AMPC)

There is something about a humble heart that attracts God's attention. God loves a humble heart, because God is also inherently humble. This means that when we portray humbleness, we are portraying God. Pride is not from the Lord.

"In your relationships with one another, have the same mindset as Christ Jesus: Who, being in very nature God, did not consider equality with God something to be used to His advantage; rather, He made Himself nothing by taking the very nature of a servant, being made human in likeness. And being found in appearance as a man, He humbled Himself by becoming obedient to death – even death on a cross!" **Philippians 2:5-8 (NIV)**

If I could tell you a story to illustrate humbling yourself, I would tell you about the time many years ago when I was working under a very difficult commander. This commander felt very insecure and threatened by me for many different reasons, and he could not let a day pass without targeting me. I was in tears every day, in fact, I began to make arrangements to transfer to another unit. Whilst making these arrangements, I prayed and asked the Lord to let His will be done. I prayed that if the Lord wanted me to transfer, then He would open the door for me. But if He didn't want me to transfer, that He would close the door. It turned out that God didn't open that door for me, and I remained under this commander. I was in great distress, but I began to pray and fast, asking the Lord to show me what the reason was that He wanted me to stay there. A few days later the Lord broke through and showed me that He wanted to teach me about submission and how to humble myself. I asked for His guidance and the Lord began to teach me the very difficult and painful process of crucifying my flesh and humbling and submitting myself to someone whom I felt was not deserving. But you see, that is the key. We must not only humble ourselves before deserving people, but humbleness must be a state of our heart, leading us to humble ourselves before *all* people, whether deserving or not. When Jesus humbled Himself and died on the cross for us, we were certainly not deserving.

The first thing I did with my commander was to buy him a Bible (I happened to know that he very much wanted one) and with it I wrote a short note apologizing for my behaviour and asking for his forgiveness – even though I felt that I had done nothing wrong. I felt that he was the unreasonable tyrant. It was a very difficult thing for me to hand him the note and the Bible the next day at work, but I did it prayerfully, because I knew it was what the Lord wanted me to do. I also wrote down five good traits of my commander that I could think of in my journal. Very resistant at first I began to meditate upon these traits every day. And I made a conscious effort to obey my commander at all times, even when I felt he was wrong (which was most of the time). In addition to this, I made a point of blessing him in my prayer time each night. At first I literally had difficulty speaking blessing over him, but each night it got easier, and easier. Slowly, but surely, our relationship began to change. He was still the stubborn tyrant, but my attitude and behaviour towards him began to change, and it changed the dynamics in our relationship. It was a slow, painful process, but the Lord began to teach me about humbling myself before people. It is a difficult process that leaves no place for self-will and pride. When you fast, always bear in mind that the most important aspect of your fast is always your heart. Your heart determines whether the Lord hears your prayers. Your humble heart can turn the Lord around to forgive you and grant you mercy, whilst your proud heart can cause the Lord to humble you, and the cleanness of your heart will draw you closer to God. The state of your heart literally determines the state of your relationship with the Lord.

"For thus says the high and lofty One-He Who inhabits eternity, Whose name is Holy: I dwell in the high and holy place, but with him also who is of a thoroughly penitent and humble spirit, to revive the spirit of the humble and to revive the heart of the thoroughly penitent [bruised with sorrow for sin]." Isaiah 57:15 (AMPC)

CHAPTER 3

SEEKING GOD *MORE*

"But if from there you will seek (inquire for and require as necessity) the Lord your God, you will find Him if you [truly] seek Him with all your heart [and mind] and soul and life."
Deuteronomy 4:29 (AMPC)

This chapter literally came forth from a series of dreams that the Lord gave me some years ago. My ministry [Daniel Ministries] has always been steeped in dreams, much like the life of Daniel in the Bible. Even before the Lord gave me my ministry, He had begun to teach me about dreams and their interpretation.

Some years ago, I began to have a series of dreams. In these dreams, the theme would always be that there is something I need to do, but I was running late. Sometimes I would dream that I need to get to work, but I was running late. The main topic throughout the dreams were always that I was late in doing something for the Lord. Each time I would wake up feeling uncomfortable. I knew that the Lord was trying to tell me something, but I didn't understand what it was. I felt that the Lord wanted me to do something for Him, but that I didn't know what it was and that I didn't have much time left. I realized that the Lord had a specific timeline in His kingdom for His children, and I was failing to meet my deadlines for the path that the Lord had me on. After each dream, I would seek the Lord in prayer about what it was that I needed to do for Him. Sometimes the Lord would show me, and other times I wouldn't get an answer. This went on for about five years.

One morning I awoke after having yet another dream of having to do something, but I was running late once again. That day I felt utterly discouraged. I got up from bed that morning, and whilst running over the dream repeatedly in my mind, I put on my exercise clothes and climbed onto my treadmill. I have always found that I have the best prayer times on my treadmill. As I began to pray, I was angry with the Lord. I told Him that He keeps giving me these dreams, and when I ask Him to show me what I needed to do, I rarely got an answer. I asked the Lord how I was supposed to do what I needed to do if He didn't speak to me and tell me. That day I had reached a tipping point, and I wasn't holding back. Suddenly the Lord answered me and spoke clearly into my spirit. It was so unexpected that it nearly brought me to a standstill. He said, *'You have been in training these past five years. I have been teaching you about a different type of dream where I guide you on what you need to do, and warn you when you are not in sync with My timeline for you. I know you feel frustrated, but I had to teach you that you need to seek Me daily about what I want you to do for Me. I am training you so that eventually you will move when I tell you to move, and do only what I tell you to do. I do not want you to do your own thing. I want you to do what I want you to do – every day. I want you to come before Me every day in prayer, and seek Me for what you need to do next. This way you will stay in My timeline for you, and you will be continually led by My Spirit. You will not be doing unnecessary things that distract you and waste time – things that are not what I have for you.'* In utter desperation I said, *'But Lord, when I ask You to show me what I need to do, why do I struggle to get an answer?'* The Lord simply answered, *'Because I want you to seek Me <u>more</u>.'*

"And commanded Judah to <u>seek the Lord</u>, the God of their fathers [<u>to inquire of and for Him and crave Him as a vital necessity</u>]..." II Chronicles 14:4 (AMPC)

Relief flooded through me as our conversation ended. I realized that (being the perfectionist that I am) I was not an utter failure. The Lord had been training me, and training can be a difficult time. A time in which we do not always understand the things that are happening to us. But suddenly it all made sense to me. That one conversation with the Lord literally changed my walk as a believer. I realized what all those dreams were about. I realized that I needed to seek the Lord every day to hear what He wanted me to do, and whilst I am doing it, I need to seek Him already for what comes next. I understood, even more so than before, that God has a timeline for everything that He wants you to do.

"See then that you walk circumspectly, not as fools but as wise, redeeming the time, because the days are evil." Ephesians 5:15-16 (NKJV)

If you procrastinate when the Lord asks something from you, then eventually it will catch up with you, and you may miss important things that the Lord has planned for you. I also understood that my dreams were a very important communication platform between the Lord and me, and I was so thankful that He was directly guiding me through these dreams. Since then many believers have come to me with similar dreams, after which I began to teach them what the Lord was teaching me. Some believers took it to heart and began to work with the Lord, while others disregarded my advice. I have found that believers who always react on the Lord's promptings (in dreams, or otherwise) grow steadily.

"For as many as are led by the Spirit of God, these are sons of God." Romans 8:14 (NKJV)

As a result of this word that the Lord spoke into my spirit, I have a habit of seeking the Lord about what He wants me to do in every area of my life. I still miss many things, and then I have dreams where the Lord warns me that I am late, and there is something He needs me to do.

At these times I will seek the Lord for a way forward, always keeping in mind His word to me, that He wants me to 'seek Him *more*'. At one such a time, I was in the process of seeking the Lord about yet another dream. I had been praying for days, and yet I had not received an answer. In desperation, I spoke to the Lord one day, and said, *'Lord, You said You want me to seek You more. I have been doing that, and yet You do not answer me!'* Immediately the Lord whispered into my ear, and said, *'I want you to fast. Part of seeking Me more, is too <u>fast</u> and seek My face.'* Once again, I learned an important lesson. I realized that when I seek the Lord and I do not get an answer, I should fast and seek Him even *more*.

"Then Jehoshaphat feared, and set himself [determinedly, as his vital need] <u>to seek the Lord; he proclaimed a fast in all Judah.</u>" II Chronicles 20:3 (AMPC)

One of the ways in which you seek God *more*, is too *fast*. Do not underestimate the power of fasting. God even tells us in His Word that we should seek Him and require Him as we require food.

"For thus says the Lord to the house of Israel: Seek Me [inquire for and of Me and require Me as you require food] and you shall live!" Amos 5:4 (AMPC)

God loves it when you seek Him more. He will sometimes wait patiently for you to seek Him *more*, so that He can spend precious time with you, and share with you what He has planned for you and what you need to do for Him.

"...the Lord is with you while you are with Him. If you seek Him [inquiring for and of Him, craving Him as your soul's first necessity], <u>He will be found by you;</u> but if you [become indifferent and] forsake Him, He will forsake you." II Chronicles 15:2 (AMPC)

As time has gone by, I have learnt so much. I realized that the things that the Lord wants me to do could be anything from a specific Bible study, or writing a book, to practical things in my life, like applying for a passport.

I have also learnt that the Lord will give me feedback on different areas in my life within my dreams. For example, if I am very obedient in doing the warfare that the Lord prompts me to do, I will get dreams where the Lord will show me how I am playing in a ball game and stopping every one of the enemy's attempts to score a goal. However, a day later, I may have a dream that I need to do something, but I am late. This simply means that in one area, I am obedient in the Lord's promptings, but in another area, I have yet to seek Him so that I don't miss something important. I have learned not to become discouraged when the Lord guides me, because I realize that it is for my own good.

Every believer in his or her lifetime will experience a need to seek the Lord. For some it may be more often than others. To seek means that you attempt to find something/someone, that you are hunting for something/someone or in the pursuit of something/someone, and even that you are *pushing towards* something/someone. When you feel the need to seek the Lord, fasting is a powerful way of pushing towards God. Fasting tells God that you are consecrating yourself to Him to seek Him more. Fasting tells God that you are willing to give up that which you need and value in your life, in order to seek Him more. Fasting tells God that, in times of need you look to *Him* for the answer. Fasting also tells God that you wish to spend more time with Him, because fasting brings with it intimate times of sharing in prayer.

When we seek God, we need to separate ourselves from the pollutions of the world:

"...all who had joined them and <u>separated themselves from the pollutions of the peoples of the land to seek the Lord,</u> the God of Israel." Ezra 6:21 (AMPC)

These pollutions may include television, or avoiding specific books or music. It may even be that we should avoid certain people.

Upon a study of the word 'seek' in the Bible I have found that we can seek God for different reasons:

- We can seek God to *inquire* of Him (Deut 4:29)
- Because we *yearn* for Him (II Chro 12:14)
- Because you require God's *presence* as your vital need (Ps 27:8)

I have also learned, through God's Word, that seeking God *more* has a specific meaning, and the Bible tells us exactly how God wants us to do this. The Bible says we must seek God:

- "[truly]…with all your heart [and mind] and soul and life" (Deut 4:29)
- With all your desire (II Chro 12:14)
- By separating yourself from all pollutions in the world (Ezra 6:21)
- By preparing and setting your heart to seek God (Ezra 7:10)
- By humbling yourself before God (Ezra 8:21)
- By seeking Him diligently (Heb 11:6)
- By seeking Him daily (Isa 58:2)
- By seeking Him with weeping (Jer 50:4)
- "seek Him by prayer and supplications, with fasting and sackcloth and ashes" (Dan 9:3)
- By seeking Him until you find Him (Matt 7:7)

Now when you seek God more, you should have only one goal in mind, and that is to *find* the Lord – meaning to find His presence where He sits on His throne. The only place you will find the Lord (if you diligently seek Him) is in His *secret place.*
"He who dwells in the <u>secret place of the Most High</u> shall remain stable and fixed under the shadow of the Almighty [Whose power no foe can withstand]" Psalm 91:1 (AMPC)

Allow me to examine this statement with you. First off, the word "secret" tells you that it is a place that is hidden, a place that is not well known and only shared confidentially with a select few. This is all true about the secret place of the Most High. This place, where God's presence is found, is hidden, and only certain chosen people are able to find it, because the path to the secret place is hidden. The whole point of seeking God more, is to enter into His secret place. In the secret place of the Most High you are protected and hidden from the enemy, because he is not able to locate you – remember, it is a *secret place.* In God's secret place is where your reward lies, where all your answers lie, and where your groundbreaking revelations lie. If you should pray and make a show in public for everyone to see, repeating meaningless words over and over, you cannot enter into the secret place of the Most High, because entry into the secret place requires seeking God with pure and sincere motives. The only way to find and enter into the secret place of the Lord is to seek Him sincerely, deeply and desperately, with a pure heart. That is the only way to God's secret place and no other path will lead you there. Even then the secret place of the Lord is not easy to find. It takes perseverance and a continual, diligent seeking of the Lord through prayer, worship and fasting. But once you have found the secret place of the Most High – once you have located it – you will know the path to the secret place of the Lord and you may visit often.

Take a look at these two Scriptures in the New Testament – one about prayer, and the other about fasting:

"But you, when you pray, go into your room, and when you have shut your door, <u>pray to your Father who is in the secret place;</u> and your Father who sees in secret will reward you openly." Matthew 6:6 (NKJV)

"But you, when you fast, anoint your head and wash your face, <u>so that you do not appear to men to be fasting, but to your Father who is in the secret place;</u> and you Father who sees in secret will reward you openly." Matthew 6:17-18 (NKJV)

In the secret place is where the Lord will make known His secrets to you in the form of revelation. When you enter into the secret place of the Most High you become a secret-keeper of the Lord. There, in heavenly places where the secret place of the Lord is found, you must enter in. There you must take hold of the secrets that the Lord shares with you (the revelations) so that you may bring them down to earth with you. You must reach out to heaven, take hold of heavenly secrets, and bring that piece of heaven down to earth with you.

"It is not [a secret laid up] in heaven, that you should say, Who shall go up for us to heaven and bring it to us, that we may hear and do it?" Deuteronomy 30:12 (AMPC)

Apostle Paul was a man that knew well the path that led to the secret place of the Lord. He travelled it often. In fact, the New Testament is riddled with all his revelations that he received from heaven and brought down to earth that we may share in those wonderful pieces of heaven.

"<u>...you have heard of the stewardship of God's grace (His unmerited favor) that was entrusted to me [to dispense to you] for your benefit, [And] that the mystery (secret) was made known to me and I was allowed to comprehend it by direct revelation...</u>" Ephesians 3:2-3 (AMPC)

Our God is the Revealer of secrets (Daniel 2:47), and if Paul learned a secret, then there was only one way to do it – he entered into the secret place of God, took hold of this secret, and brought it down to this earth with him.

"<u>I have learned in any and all circumstances the secret of facing every situation,</u> whether well-fed or going hungry, having sufficiency and enough to spare or going without and being in want." Philippians 4:12 (AMPC)

This is a beautiful example of the apostle Paul laying hold of the secret of facing any and all circumstances – a revelation from God Himself.

Now an important fact about a secret is that it *always* carries a lot of weight. Hence the reason for it being kept a secret. Secrets can, therefore, do much harm should it end up in the wrong hands. However, when a secret ends up in the right hands, a good secret can accomplish miracles and is worth more than gold. When the Lord reveals a secret to you, it will always be something important, something that can potentially change your life and that of your family, depending on what you do with the secret. The secret-keeper of God's secrets must believe when God reveals a secret to him. In fact, he must believe so much that he goes forth and acts in faith as he implements what was revealed to him in heaven. Only then will the true value of the secret be revealed.

"The secret things belong unto the Lord our God, <u>but the things which are revealed belong to us and to our children forever</u>..." Deuteronomy 29:29 (AMPC)

When the Lord reveals His secrets to you, you must take hold of those revealed secrets and you must treasure each of them as a gift from God, because that gift from God has now become an inheritance for your children. You must treasure each revelation, look after it, hold on to it, keep it close to your heart at all times, and implement it, because it has been given to you and to your children forever.

My sincere prayer is that this chapter inspires you to seek God *more*, to push towards Him until you find Him, to seek Him daily and to seek Him with fasting and prayer until you reach the secret place of the Most High in heavenly places. May you take hold of every secret that the Lord wishes to impart to you. May you keep those secrets close to your heart, live them in your life, and may they become a rich inheritance to your children forever.

CHAPTER 4

ACTIVELY FASTING

"And don't forget to do good and to share with those in need. These are the sacrifices that please God." Hebrews 13:16 (NLT)

For the first few years after being born-again I fasted as I believed fasting should be done. I read many books on the subject to educate myself as best I could, and whatever I found to be sound doctrine I practiced. As the years progressed the Lord began to teach *me* about fasting. Pretty soon I began to practice the principles that the Lord taught me about fasting, too. As I was obedient to put into practice the principles that the Lord showed me, He began to increase His revelations towards me. About a year ago I was studying the topic of fasting in the Bible as the Lord led me, when He began to reveal to me a different side to fasting that revolutionized my concept of the practice altogether.

When believers hear the word 'fast' you immediately think about abstaining from food, or water, or something that is important to you – the main word in this sentence being 'abstain'. As believers we think that fasting and abstaining are synonym. However, the Lord has taught me that fasting is a sacrifice, and you do not only sacrifice by abstaining, but you can also sacrifice by *actively doing something*. Did you know that Biblically fasting does not only require you to abstain from something, but equally (maybe even more so) it requires you to actively do something? What if, when you plan and set the perimeters of your fast, you not only decide what you will abstain from, but also what you will be actively doing for your fast? Sometimes that which you do forms the greater sacrifice.

In Isaiah 58 (the famous fasting chapter in the Bible) the Lord is speaking to the Israelites about fasting. Firstly, the Lord asks Isaiah the prophet to lift up his voice like a trumpet.

"Cry aloud, spare not. Lift up your voice like a trumpet and declare to My people their transgression and to the house of Jacob their sins!" Isaiah 58:1 (AMPC)

What exactly does that mean? One of the reasons a trumpet was blown in Biblical times, was to warn the Israelites of impending danger. In fact, this has been the practice down the centuries. The term 'whistle-blower' comes from law enforcement officials in the 19th century who used a whistle to alert the public or other police officers to danger. Even in sports referees use whistle-blowing to get everyone's attention in order to indicate any illegal or foul play. When the Lord asked Isaiah the prophet to lift up his voice like a trumpet, He was in effect saying to Isaiah, *'Speak, and warn the people of their transgressions and my impending judgment.'* Through Isaiah the prophet God warned the Israelites about His impending judgment, and He makes it very clear that the Israelites' fasts were not sufficient to stave off His judgment. God felt that their fasts were no longer acceptable to Him, thus His ears were closed to their prayers.

"Yet they seek, inquire for, and require Me daily and <u>delight [externally] to know My ways,</u> as [if they were in reality] a nation that did righteousness and forsook not the ordinance of their God. They ask of Me righteous judgments, <u>they delight to draw near to God [in visible ways].</u> Why have we fasted, they say, and You do not see it? Why have we afflicted ourselves, and You take no knowledge [of it]? Behold [O Israel], on the day of your fast [when you should be grieving for your sins]...[The facts are that] you fast only for strife and debate and to smite with the fist of wickedness. <u>Fasting as you do today will not cause your voice to be heard on high."</u> Isaiah 58:2-4 (AMPC)

When the Lord speaks to the Israelites He clearly indicates to them that their hearts are not right before Him, and therefore their prayers will not be heard. Remember that the Lord looks at the heart. When the Lord looked at their hearts He did not find humble, penitent hearts surrendering to Him. The Lord found that they "delight [externally]" to know His ways – clearly meaning that this delight to know His ways were not from their hearts. It was all a big, public show. They were merely drawing near to God in "visible ways" (outwardly for everyone to see) which was of no interest to the Lord. God saw through their whole charade, because He knows the secrets of the heart.

"If we had forgotten the name of our God or stretched out our hands to a strange god, Would not God discover this? <u>For He knows the secrets of the heart</u>." Psalm 44:20-21 (AMPC)

The Lord then continues by telling them the type of fast that *He* has chosen, and therefore the type of fast that is acceptable to Him.

"[Rather] is not this the fast that I have chosen...Is it not to divide your bread with the hungry and bring the homeless poor into your house-when you see the naked, that you cover him, and that you hide not yourself from [the needs of] your own flesh and blood?...If you take away from your midst yokes of oppression [wherever you find them], the finger pointed in scorn [toward the oppressed or the godly], and every form of false, harsh, unjust, and wicked speaking, And if you pour out that with which you sustain your own life for the hungry and satisfy the need of the afflicted..." Isaiah 58:6-7; 9-10 (AMPC)

Taking this Scripture into account, let's take a look at some additional ways of fasting that are acceptable to the Lord and includes *doing something* as a sacrifice, in addition to abstaining from something:

- Verse 7 tells you to *"divide your bread with the hungry"*: What if, when you fast, you consciously divide every meal in two and give half of every meal away to someone in need as a way of fasting?

- Verse 7 says you should *"bring the homeless poor into your house "*: What if, when you fast, you invite someone poor into your home for a good meal and share the Gospel with them?

- Verse 7 also says that *"when you see the naked, that you cover him"*: What if, as a way of fasting you give away a piece of clothing to someone in need every day?

- Lastly, verse 7 says to *"hide not yourself from [the needs of] your own flesh and blood"*: What if, when you fast you also look to the needs of your own flesh and blood? This does not necessarily refer only to material things. What if, during your fast you took one hour every day to do something special with a family member? Maybe you could take your grandmother, who struggles to drive, shopping for some much needed articles? Maybe you could assist your elderly father, who struggles with his back, to cut the grass in his garden? Maybe you could take over cooking from your wife for one night to give her a chance to tend to something personal she never gets the time for? Maybe you could take the trash out for your husband when he comes home late and tired from work? There are so many ways in which you could actively *do something* (and thereby make a sacrifice) during your fast to make life easier for your family.

- Verse 9 says to *"take away from your midst ... every form of false, harsh, unjust, and wicked speaking"*: What if, as a way of fasting you make it a point to speak only uplifting and edifying words about others? Instead of concentrating on *abstaining* from speaking false, harsh, unjust, and wicked words, why not rather focus on the good traits of others and make it a point to speak edifying and uplifting words over them? Let's be honest, are you so holy that you never say a wrong word about someone else? To start monitoring the words that you speak about others will begin to make you aware how many times you actually do have false, harsh, unjust and wicked words to say about other people. Maybe this could eventually lead to a 'word fast' becoming a way of life, instead of only a fast for a mere few days. On the other hand, when you consciously look for something good to say about each person, it changes your mind-set. You begin to focus and recognize the good in every person. Every person in this world has positive qualities.

- Verse 9 says you should *"take away from your midst… the finger pointed in scorn [toward the oppressed or the godly]"*: What if, when others around you gossip or slander, you in turn find the positive in that person and boldly speak it out? Do you know what slander is? Slander is to rob someone of their honour. Will you take a stand in the midst of others, and bravely remove the finger pointed in scorn to the oppressed or the godly? Will you manage to do this in love?

- Verse 10 tells you to *"pour out that with which you sustain your own life for the hungry and satisfy the need of the afflicted"*: What if, as a way of fasting you take one main meal every day, wrap it up, and go into the streets and give it to someone in need?

Clearly, fasting is not merely to *abstain* as a means of sacrifice, but also to *actively do something*. There are so many ways in which you can sacrifice by doing something to help others when you fast. You could offer to clean your church, or help out at the Sunday-school.

You can pay for someone's groceries at the till when you see they are in need.

"Do not forget or neglect to do kindness and good, to be generous and distribute and contribute to the needy [of the church as embodiment and proof of fellowship], for such sacrifices are pleasing to God." Hebrews 13:16 (AMPC)

Alternatively, you could get up for one extra hour each night (in addition to your usual prayer time), for a time of exclusive thanksgiving and worship – no warfare and no petition-prayers – making it all bout God.

"Through Him, therefore, let us constantly and at all times <u>offer up to God a sacrifice of praise, which is the fruit of the lips that thankfully acknowledge and confess and glorify His name.</u>" Hebrews 13:15 (AMPC)

The whole point will be, that when you regularly practice these principles it will begin to stick and become a way of life instead of merely a fast for a few days. *That will be pleasing to God.*

CHAPTER 5

FASTING THROUGH MOURNING

"Therefore also now, says the Lord, turn and keep on coming to Me with all your heart, with fasting, with weeping, and with mourning [until every hindrance is removed and the broken fellowship is restored]." Joel 2:12 (AMPC)

In the Bible you will find many Scriptures that reveal to you how the Lord comforts those who mourn, and restores joy to them.

"To proclaim the acceptable year of the Lord [the year of His favour] and the day of vengeance of our God, <u>to comfort all who mourn, to grant [consolation and joy] to those who mourn in Zion</u> – to give them an ornament (a garland or diadem) of beauty instead of ashes, <u>the oil of joy instead of mourning, the garment [expressive] of praise instead of a heavy, burdened, and failing spirit</u>..." Isaiah 61:2-3 (AMPC)

When you read through the Word of God there is an increasing awareness that God always reaches out to those who mourn. In the Book of Daniel we find this interesting account:

"In those days I, Daniel, was mourning for three whole weeks. I ate no pleasant bread or desirable food, nor did any meat or wine come into my mouth; and I did not anoint myself at all for three full weeks." Daniel 10:2-3 (AMPC)

Now, it is interesting to note that at this time when Daniel was mourning, he was not mourning for someone who had died. It is customary when someone dies that one may mourn the person who has passed away.

"And Sarah died in Kiriath-arba, that is, Hebron, in the land of Canaan. <u>And Abraham went to mourn for Sarah and to weep for her</u>." Genesis 23:2 (AMPC)

When you look at the meaning of the word mourning you will find that mourning is an expression of sorrow over someone's death. Yet, here was Daniel, great man of God, mourning when no one had died. I have come to understand over the years that mourning, in the Bible, can also be a type of a fast. One can mourn over a loved one's death, and one can mourn before God in fasting.

As I studied the topic of mourning in God's Word, I became increasingly aware that mourning is an outward reflection of one's inner heart. When you mourn over a loved one's death, the pain cuts deeply into your heart and you will find that this pain in your heart will affect the way that you act. You may lose your appetite, on the day of the burial you may wear black to show how dark your sorrow is, you may weep with tears flowing and you may not sleep much at night. These are all merely outward signs of how a person's death may affect you.

In the Book of Daniel 10:2-3 Daniel was clearly mourning, but he was mourning *as a way of fasting*. In this Scripture Daniel says that he "ate no pleasant bread or desirable food, nor did any meat or wine" come into his mouth. Daniel fasted from specific foods to reveal to the Lord how deep his mourning affected his heart – through abstaining from specific foods, Daniel showed the Lord the *condition* of his heart. Now I know there have been many books written on the Daniel fast and all the many foods that you must refrain from. However, after much study I have humbly decided to change my approach to a "Daniel fast" (which is in fact a mourning).

In the beginning, when I practiced a Daniel fast I was very much focused on the type of foods I could eat and should not eat. After some years, I felt an increasing need to change my approach to this fast.

I felt that I was so focused on my diet that the reasons for my fast got lost in the process. I wanted to focus more on the *reason* for my fast, and less on the *food*. So I took a closer look at this Scripture in the Book of Daniel, and I realized that the behaviour that Daniel exhibited was similar to that of a person who was mourning. When you think about it logically, a person who truly mourns a loved one's death does not eat pleasant bread or desirable food, because they would have lost their appetite. In fact, they would probably not want to drink wine either, as wine may have the connotation to celebration – which is the exact opposite of how a person in true mourning may feel. I felt that I understood what Daniel was doing when he undertook his "mourning". He ate as someone would who had no appetite.

Like I said, this changed my approach to a mourning. I decided that I was going to imitate the behaviour of someone who was mourning. I was going to abstain from pleasant bread and desirable food. As a rule I do not drink any alcohol, but I decided to stay away from anything that would seem like comfort food e.g. anything with sugar (including cakes and bakes), coffee (if it makes you happy), and bread and pasta. This led to me giving more attention to the reason for my mourning, than the actual food I was eating.

I also realized that a mourning was so much more than just abstaining from specific foods. A mourning is all about the heart (which is what God looks at), and about showing God your heart. A mourning is also about the way you act, and the way you speak. As I studied the topic of mourning in the Bible I came across specific behaviours that people would exhibit when they were in mourning. People in mourning would:

1. Rend (tear) their clothes as a sign of how torn apart their hearts were with sadness (II Samuel 3:31)
2. Eat the bread of mourning (Ezekiel 24:16-17)
3. Put on sackcloth and lie in ashes (Esther 4:3)

4. Bury the person who had died (I Kings 13:29
5. Weep (Nehemiah 8:9)/ Have tears flowing down their cheeks (Ezekiel 24:16-17)
6. Remove their shoes (Ezekiel 24:17)
7. Sit on the ground/in ashes (Isaiah 3:26)
8. Fail to look up (Isaiah 38:14)
9. Cry out (Jeremiah 48:31)
10. Beat their breast (Matthew 24:30)
11. Not wear any jewellery (Exodus 33:4)
12. Bow down (Psalm 35:14)
13. Dress in black (Jeremiah 14:2)
14. Not care to attend social celebrations (*my own input*)

(All Scriptures mentioned above are from the AMPC version)
The Bible also mentions that Daniel did not anoint himself during his mourning for three whole weeks.
"...and I did not anoint myself at all for the full three weeks."
Daniel 10:3 (AMPC)
In Biblical times people anointed themselves with oil as it was used much more as perfume than an actual oil. Anointing yourself with fragrant oil was also a sign of joy. Therefore, not anointing yourself at all was a sign of grief. By not anointing himself with fragrant oil, Daniel was further indicating to the Lord the extent of his grief as he mourned.
Being fully aware that you are not to make an outward show to others around you that you are fasting, I looked at these above-mentioned behaviours logically, and realized that most of them can be incorporated in a mourning without making a show to those around you that you are in fact in a type of fast. For example, you have the loss of appetite (eating the bread of mourning) which will include abstaining from specific pleasant and desirable foods. Then you have weeping. Have you ever prayed so deeply about something that is laying heavily on your heart that you wept with tears flowing down your cheeks as you prayed?

Does that not clearly indicate the condition of your heart to the Lord? Removing your shoes, sitting down on the ground (even kneeling or bowing), and failing to look up can be done when you are in your private prayer closet, in deep conversation with the Lord.

"But <u>when you pray, go into your [most] private room, and, closing the door, pray to your Father,</u> Who is in secret; and your Father, Who sees in secret, will reward you in the open." Matthew 6:6 (AMPC)

The condition of your heart is for your Father to see, not for everyone. So, when you go into you private prayer closet and have closed the door, you may show Him the physical signs that you are mourning to reveal the condition of your heart. Here in your prayer closet you may *cry out* to the Lord about the things you are fasting for. You may weep with tears flowing down your cheeks and beat your breast as you bring your petitions before the Lord.

It is interesting to note that the New Testament also connects mourning with fasting. Take a look at these Words spoken by Jesus:

"Then the disciples of John came to Jesus, inquiring, Why is it that we and the Pharisees fast often, [that is, abstain from food and drink as a religious exercise], but Your disciples do not fast? And Jesus replied to them, Can the wedding guests <u>mourn</u> while the bridegroom is still with them? The days will come when the bridegroom is taken away from them, and then they will fast." Matthew 9:14-15 (AMPC)

Now that we have established that mourning is a type of a fast, you should also understand that there are specific reasons why one should undertake a mourning as a fast. Let's take a look at reasons why people in the Bible mourned – relating to reasons you should undertake a mourning of a fast:

- You may mourn when you complain to or petition God for something (Ps 55:2; Isa 38:14; Ps 88:9)
- When the wicked bears rule (Prov 29:2)

- Mourn over the spiritual condition of your city (Isa 66:10)
- When God has passed judgment and you seek mercy (Jer 4:28; Ex 33:4; Neh 1:4)
- When you repent for your sins (Jas 4:8-10; Ezra 10:6)
- To restore the broken fellowship between you and God (Joel 2:12-14)

For me personally, one of the most important reasons to undertake a mourning is the repentance of sins in order to draw nearer to God.

"Draw near to God and He will draw near to you. Cleanse your hands, you sinners; and purify your hearts, you double-minded. Lament and mourn and weep! Let your laughter be turned into mourning and your joy to gloom." James 4:8-9 (NKJV)

When you purify your heart and cleanse your hands it speaks of repentance and getting rid of sin in your life. When you do this it helps you, firstly, to be able to run your race as a believer without hindrance.

"Therefore then, since we are surrounded by so great a cloud of witnesses [who have borne testimony to the Truth], let us strip off and throw aside every encumbrance (unnecessary weight) and that sin which so readily (deftly and cleverly) clings to and entangles us, and let us run with patient endurance and steady and active persistence the appointed course of the race that is set before us" Hebrews 12:1 (AMPC)

Secondly, it has the benefit of removing the sin which stands between you and God and thereby you are able to draw nearer to the Lord. However, removing sin *always* starts with repentance. You must first repent for committing sin in your life. Have you ever heard the saying that acknowledging the fact that you have a problem is the first step to healing?

It is exactly how it works with sin in your life. You first have to acknowledge the fact that you have a problem in a specific area, before healing in that area can begin. This may sound simple, but take into consideration the fact that many people do not believe that they struggle with a specific problem, when, in fact, they actually do. Many believers are blind to their own actions and sin. It takes revelation from the Holy Spirit to reveal to you that you have sin in your life. I have met so many believers who struggle with resentment and unforgiveness, yet they freely proclaim that they have no problem in this area. This is mostly not because they are hypocritical, but because they are in the dark and genuinely do not realize that they struggle in that area. It takes intervention from the Holy Spirit to reveal this to them. It takes the Lord to shine His light on that area in their lives so that the sin can come into the light. Only when true realization sets in and you begin to see the destruction that this sin is sowing in your life, can you truly begin to turn from that sin. True repentance comes from a very deep place within your heart. A place where you have grown to hate that sin and its effects in your life and those closest to you. That is when you begin to fast and mourn. You mourn for the hold that this sin has had over your life. You mourn for how you have sinned against the Lord. You mourn for the distance this sin has placed between you and the Lord. You mourn for how this sin is affecting your testimony in your walk with God. You lose your appetite. You struggle to sleep at night, because the desperate desire to get rid of this sin keeps you up and makes you restless. You go into your prayer closet, close the door, take off your shoes, and kneel down in prayer whilst you beat your breast and weep with tears flowing down your cheeks as you cry out to God to forgive you and to deliver you from sinning anymore against Him. *That is true mourning from the heart.*

"[As you draw near to God] be deeply penitent and grieve, even weep [over your disloyalty]. Let your laughter be turned to grief and your mirth to dejection and heartfelt shame [for your sins]." James 4:9 (AMPC)

That is the mourning that believers should engage in as you mourn for the sin in your life – desperate for God's restoration. That is the mourning that the Lord calls us to.

"And in that day the Lord God of hosts called you to weeping and mourning, to the shaving off of all your hair [in humiliation] and to the girding with sackcloth." Isaiah 22:12 (AMPC)

Like I said in the beginning of the chapter: People mourn when someone has died. In that respect we are not really that different. We mourn and turn from sin, and in the process of our mourning our old man of sin dies.

"knowing this, that our old man was crucified with Him, that the body of sin might be done away with, that we should no longer be slaves of sin. For he who has died has been freed from sin." Romans 6:6-7 (NKJV)

When you recognize sin in your life and you are desperate to turn away from it, and desperate for God's restoration, it is proper to undertake a mourning as a way of fasting. My prayer is that this chapter will not only motivate you to seek the Holy Spirit about the hidden sin in your life, but that it will also inspire you to undertake a mourning as you reveal your heart to the Lord in repentance.

CHAPTER 6

THE SABBATH

"[Earnestly] remember the Sabbath day, to keep it holy (withdrawn from common employment and dedicated to God). Six days you shall labor and do all your work, but the seventh day is a Sabbath to the Lord you God; in it you shall not do any work, you, or your son, your daughter, your manservant, your maidservant, your domestic animals, or the sojourner within your gates. For in six days the Lord made the heavens and the earth, the sea, and all that is in them, and rested the seventh day. That is why the Lord blessed the Sabbath day and hallowed it [set it apart for His purposes]."
Exodus 20:8-11 (AMPC)

Did you know that the Lord sees the Sabbath as a fast? I learned this important piece of information as the Lord began to reveal His secrets to me about fasting. The Lord had been unpacking Isaiah Chapter 58 to me (the famous fasting chapter) and within it He began to show me that the Sabbath is also a fast. I learned not only that the Sabbath is a fast, but I also learned that it differs from other fasts.

"Behold [O Israel], on the day of your fast [when you should be grieving for your sins], you find profit in your business, and [instead of stopping all work, as the law implies you and your workmen should do] you extort from your hired servants a full amount of labor." Isaiah 58:3 (AMPC)

You may be asking yourself how a Sabbath fast may be different. Well, in a normal fast you get to choose for yourself what you wish to abstain from, what you will actively do, as well as how you spend your day and maintain your fast.

However, a Sabbath fast (which typically takes place on the seventh day of the week) is different. For a Sabbath fast God has given you specific guidelines in the Bible on how to spend your day on your fast, what you should abstain from, and what you should be doing on that day. The Sabbath is a fast that is very important to the Lord. Therefore, it is a fast that God has specifically chosen *for* you, and He did so having you in mind.

"...it is a sign between Me and you throughout your generations, that you may know that I, the Lord, sanctify you [set you apart for Myself]." Exodus 31:13 (AMPC)

When you partake in a Sabbath fast, it shows that you are God's child. It shows that you are different from the world, because you set a day aside to honour God and spend intimate time with Him. As you partake in this fast, it is a sign that God is sanctifying you. Only God's children (His chosen ones) will hear His call to a Sabbath fast and honour it.

"[Earnestly] remember the Sabbath day, to keep it holy (withdrawn from common employment and dedicated to God). Six days you shall labor and do all your work, but the seventh day is a Sabbath to the Lord you God; in it you shall not do any work, you, or your son, your daughter, your manservant, your maidservant, your domestic animals, or the sojourner within your gates. For in six days the Lord made the heavens and the earth, the sea, and all that is in them, and rested the seventh day. That is why the Lord blessed the Sabbath day and hallowed it [set it apart for His purposes]."
Exodus 20:8-11 (AMPC)

The Sabbath day (other than any other day) is a day that the Lord has set apart for His Own purposes. On that specific day, the Lord wants His children to become a part of that purpose, and not do their own thing like any other day of the week, because it is *His* day.

Now, before we go any further, let's explore the meaning of the word "Sabbath". The Hebrew word for Sabbath means intermission, it means to take a pause or a break, and it refers to an interval between parts. In reality, the Lord wants us to take a Sabbath fast as a break between our weeks. It is a day in which the Lord wants us to pause, look away from the world and all its distractions, and focus solely on Him and our relationship with Him. It is the type of fast that will refuel you, and build you up spiritually, so that you are able to start your new week refreshed and Spirit-filled. Have you ever started a week on a Monday and felt that you are tired and you cannot face your week? A Sabbath will address all those symptoms.

I have done an extensive study on the Sabbath fast in the Bible, and during this fast I have found that there were certain key words that kept popping up in relation to a Sabbath fast. Here is what I have found:

1. <u>Rest:</u>

"The Lord said, Tomorrow is a solemn <u>rest</u>, a holy Sabbath to the Lord." Exodus 16:23 (AMPC)
The Lord sees the Sabbath as a day of physical and spiritual rest. It is not only a day wherein to rest physically, but as you spend time with the Lord on your day you are in effect also resting and refreshing your spirit man.

2. <u>Holy:</u>

"The Lord said, Tomorrow is a solemn rest, a <u>holy</u> Sabbath to the Lord." Exodus 16:23 (AMPC)
The word "holy" is a word that refers to being dedicated and consecrated to the Lord. God sees the Sabbath as a holy day in which He wants you to dedicate the day to Him and His purposes. God wants you to set apart the Sabbath for Him alone every week.

On that day He wants to be first and foremost on your "to do" list.

3. <u>Sanctify:</u>

"...it is a sign between Me and you throughout your generations, that you may know that I, the Lord, <u>sanctify</u> you [set you apart for Myself]." Exodus 31:13 (AMPC)
The word "sanctify" is a word that refers to being purified and set free from sin. On the Sabbath the Lord wants you to take time to do some soul searching. It is a day in which the Lord wants you to ask the Holy Spirit to search your heart so that you may have a time of repentance for the past week. It is a day in which the blood of Jesus will wash you and sanctify you.
"If we [freely] admit that we have sinned and confess our sins, He is faithful and just (true to His own nature and promises) and will forgive our sins [dismiss our lawlessness] and [continuously] cleanse us from all unrighteousness [everything not in conformity to His will in purpose, thought, and action]." I John 1:9 (AMPC)

4. <u>Refreshed:</u>

"It is a sign between Me and the Israelites forever; for in six days the Lord made the heavens and earth, and on the seventh day He ceased and was <u>refreshed</u>." Exodus 31:17 (AMPC)
The word "refreshed" refers to a person who has gained strength and energy. The Sabbath is a day designed for you to regain your spiritual strength and energy for the coming week. A *weak* believer cannot stand in the day of evil and face his enemy, but a *refreshed* believer will have the courage, strength and energy to do so.

"Finally, my brethren, be strong in the Lord and in the power of His might. Put on the whole armor of God, that you may be able to stand against the wiles of the devil." Ephesians 6:10-11 (NKJV)

5. Assembly:

"Six days shall work be done, but the seventh day is the Sabbath of rest, a holy convocation or assembly by summons." Leviticus 23:3 (AMPC)

The word "assembly" refers to a group of people gathered together in one place for a common purpose – which sounds a lot like church to me! The Sabbath is a day for believers to gather in churches where you are fed with the Bread of life and where you can honour and celebrate God together as a family.

Now, quite early in this chapter I mentioned that the Sabbath fast is different from other fasts in that the Lord has specific requirements for you on that day. These are the requirements that I could gather in my own study about the Sabbath fast:

1. Abstain from work:

On the Sabbath God wants us to abstain from physical work in order to spend our time with Him. I have learned through experience that this abstaining from physical work is not only for us to rest physically. I have realized that doing physical work on the Sabbath distracts your attention and focus from the Lord. Your focus is more on the work you are doing, whereas God wants you to sit quietly with Him, focus on Him, and listen for His voice. The voice of the Holy Spirit can sometimes be the softest whisper, and if you do not cut out the world and all its distractions, you may miss it.

The Sabbath is the time where you can quietly sit before the Lord and catch up for any time during the week you may have missed the direction of the Holy Spirit in His still, gentle voice. God will also not take kindly to it if you expect people under your employment to work on a Sabbath, because, in essence, you are keeping them from spending time with Him.

"Why have we fasted, they say, and You do not see it? Why have we afflicted ourselves, and You take no knowledge [of it]? Behold [O Israel], on the day of your fast [when you should be grieving for your sins], you find profit in your business, and [instead of stopping all work, as the law implies you and your workmen should do] you extort from your hired servants a full amount of labor." Isaiah 58:3 (AMPC)

At the same time I want to caution you to not become legalistic about the Sabbath fast. The Sabbath is not a set of rules, but more a way of life that the Lord wishes you to adopt on this day.

"So let no one judge you in food or in drink, or regarding a festival or a new moon or Sabbaths, which are a shadow of things to come, but the substance is of Christ." Colossians 2:16-17 (NKJV)

Instead, let us learn from the Israelites who consciously prepared for the Sabbath:

"It was the day of Preparation [for the Sabbath], and the Sabbath was dawning (approaching)." Luke 23:54 (AMPC)

The Israelites had a habit of preparing for the Sabbath so that they could rest on that day and give all their attention to the Lord, the way He wanted them to.

2. <u>Abstain from spiritual warfare and physical exercise:</u>

"For physical training is of some value (useful for a little), but godliness (spiritual training) is useful and of value in everything and in every way, for it holds promise for the present life and also for the life which is to come." I Timothy 4:8 (AMPC)

In this instance, I feel the need to share a testimony with you that happened to me some years ago. It was a Sunday morning, and for some reason (which I fail to remember at this point), I was unable to attend church that morning. As I lay in bed, I began to run through my mind what I was going to do with my day. The first thing I thought of doing was to get dressed and spend some time on my treadmill in warfare. Immediately as I thought about this, the Lord spoke clearly into my spirit and said, *"No, you do not exercise on a Sabbath. It is a day of rest."* Now, understand me: it is very relaxing for me to get onto my treadmill. It is the place where I have powerful times of prayer. I have experienced the presence of the Lord on my treadmill many times. However, I realized that, as relaxing as I found it; the Lord did not want me to exercise on my treadmill on a Sabbath. As I heard the Lord's voice, I began to change my plans for the day. I decided that I would not exercise, but that I was definitely going to have a time of warfare. Immediately the Lord spoke to me again, and said, *"No, you also do not do warfare on a Sabbath."* I realized that the type of prayer the Lord wants you to engage in on a Sabbath is not the warfare type, but rather the quiet, intimate, repenting type of prayer in His presence. He wants your attention and He wants to spend quality time with His child. The Sabbath is family time with your Father.

3. <u>Actively sanctify your heart:</u>

"So repent (change your mind and purpose); turn around and return [to God], that your sins may be erased (blotted out, wiped clean)..."Acts 3:19 (AMPC)

The Sabbath is a day on which you speak to the Holy Spirit and ask Him to search your heart deeply. Then set aside a time of prayer where you can actively respond to the promptings of the Holy Spirit as He reveals to you what is in your heart. Repent not only for sins committed, but also for things omitted each week – that which the Lord wanted you to do, but which you failed in doing. Forgive whoever needs to be forgiven, set the wrong motives right in your heart, and if someone has taken an offense against you – *set it right.*

4. <u>Actively do those things that honour God:</u>

"<u>If you turn away</u> your foot from [traveling unduly on] the Sabbath, <u>from doing your own pleasure on My holy day, and call the Sabbath a [spiritual] delight</u>, the holy day of the Lord honourable, <u>and honor Him and it, not going your own way or seeking or finding your own pleasure or speaking with your own [idle] words</u>" Isaiah 58:13 (AMPC)
"And do not carry a burden out of your houses on the Sabbath day or do any work, but <u>keep the Sabbath day holy (set apart to the worship of God)</u>, as I commanded your fathers." Jeremiah 17:22 (AMPC)
Make the Sabbath a day of going to church to honour and celebrate God. Spend time in prayer, worship, thanksgiving, etc. Do not do "your own pleasure" as the Scripture warns us. Watching television or playing games the whole day is not the type of rest that the Lord had in mind when He instituted the Sabbath fast. God loves it when you seek His face and spend intimate time with Him in prayer.

5. <u>Actively guard over the words that you speak:</u>

"If you turn away…from…speaking with your own [idle] words" Isaiah 58:13 (AMPC)

On the Sabbath even our choice of words matter to the Lord. The word "idle" refers to something being pointless and without any purpose. Our words, rather than using them for pointless discussions that have no purpose, should be used in thanksgiving, prayer and the worship of the Lord. God listens to every word that we speak.

"__Then those who feared the Lord talked often one to another; and the Lord listened and heard it,__ and a book of remembrance was written before Him of those who reverenced and worshipfully feared the Lord and who thought on His name. And they shall be Mine, says the Lord of hosts, in that day when I publicly recognize and openly declare them to be My jewels (My special possession, My peculiar treasure). And I will spare them, as a man spares his own son who serves him." Malachi 3:16-17 (AMPC)

In effect, the Sabbath fast is a way of honouring God through seeking His face in prayer, worship, thanksgiving, resting, sanctifying your heart, and doing and saying things that honour God. Your focus should be on the Lord and on honouring *Him* on this day without any distractions from the world.

Remember: God created the Sabbath with you in mind – He created it *for you*. Do not become legalistic and lose sight of the Sabbath's purpose.

"And Jesus said to them, The Sabbath was made on account and for the sake of man, not man for the Sabbath. So the Son of Man is Lord even of the Sabbath." Mark 2:27-28 (AMPC)

God is your Creator, and as such, He knows exactly what you need to function in His kingdom. Many believers complain about being tired, overwhelmed, not able to cope, burned out, and not having enough time with the Lord. The Lord for this very reason created the Sabbath fast. If you keep the Sabbath in a way that honour's God all these issues will be addressed on a weekly basis.

The Lord knows that time in His presence will refresh you, giving you new strength for what you may face in the coming week.

"Repent therefore and be converted, that your sins may be blotted out, so that times of refreshing may come from the presence of the Lord" Acts 3:19 (NKJV)

CHAPTER 7

FASTING TO BREAK BONDAGES

"[Rather] is not this the fast that I have chosen: to loose the bonds of wickedness, to undo the bands of the yoke, to let the oppressed go free, and that you break every [enslaving] yoke?"
Isaiah 58:6 (AMPC)

Fasting is a very powerful way to break bondages and gain deliverance. In fact, in some cases your deliverance breakthrough may be unnecessarily delayed *unless* you fast.
"But this kind does not go out except by prayer and fasting."
Matthew 17:21 (AMPC)
Now I know that there has been so much written about this one little Scripture in the Bible, and so many different explanations given. I have even heard people say that this Scripture should be excluded from the Bible. This is my personal take on the latter:
"All Scripture is given by inspiration of God, and is profitable for doctrine, for reproof, for correction, for instruction in righteousness, that the man of God may be complete, thoroughly equipped for every good work." II Timothy 3:16-17 (NKJV)
The Lord has used this Scripture extensively in my life. It started many years ago in a prayer room at my work place one warm afternoon. We were having a powerful prayer and worship session, and as we began to go deeper into the Spirit, a close friend and colleague of mine began to manifest. This came totally unexpected. However, I was not new to the concept of deliverance and I immediately began to go through the motions.

It was a very stubborn spirit, and it took some time that day for my friend to gain her deliverance. As the deliverance progressed the spirit revealed itself to be an Incubus spirit. In all my previous experience with these types of spirits, I had found them to be very stubborn and not easy to gain deliverance from. In fact, about a year previous to that day it had taken me months of prayer and warfare to gain my own deliverance from an Incubus spirit. As my colleague gained her deliverance, the Lord spoke to me very clearly. He reminded me that she was on day eighteen of her 21-day fast. Then the Lord clearly gave me the Scripture in Matthew 17:21. He said, *"Some spirits are stubborn, and if you want deliverance from them, then you need to release more power through fasting."* That has been a platform on which the Lord has built extensively in my life. Through the years, the Lord has built a list for me of strong, stubborn spirits that requires you to fast when you seek deliverance from them.

When it comes to deliverance, fasting is the way to release more power in the spirit, because fasting is so powerful that it breaks bondages and weakens the enemy, while strengthening your own spirit man. Your spirit man gains strength, because during a fast you are denying your flesh and focusing on the Lord as prayer and worship typically increases. This, coupled with the fact that the power that you are releasing in the spirit weakens the enemy, eventually leads to bondages being broken.

"For the flesh desires what is contrary to the Spirit, and the Spirit what is contrary to the flesh. They are in conflict with each other..." Galatians 5:17 (NIV)

In my life the Lord has not only delivered me from bondages as I fasted, but He usually teaches me at length about each bondage as I pray and fast against it.

"Is not this the fast that I have chosen: To loose the bonds of wickedness, to undo the heavy burdens, to let the oppressed go free, and that you break every yoke?" Isaiah 58:6 (NKJV)

I believe that one of the reasons that fasting was given to us, is because it is so powerful for deliverance. This Scripture speaks of different kinds of oppression that fasting and prayer is able to break. The first part, 'To loose the bonds of wickedness", speaks about soul ties which I will discuss at length a little later in the chapter. It also takes me back to the woman that Jesus healed in the temple:

"So ought not this woman, being a daughter of Abraham, <u>whom Satan has bound</u> – think of it – for eighteen years, <u>be loosed from this bond</u> on the Sabbath?" Luke 13:16 (NKJV)

This woman was bound by a wicked spirit of infirmity (Luke 13:12). Isaiah 58:6 tells us that strong spirits of infirmity (physical or mental illness or weakness) can be dealt with by prayer and fasting.

Now when we speak of the second part, "to undo the heavy burdens", I believe that this Scripture refers to a *spirit of heaviness*. The Scripture clearly shows us that fasting can deal with this spirit of heaviness that places heavy burdens on us – burdens that we are not equipped to deal with.

"To console those who mourn (remember that mourn is also a fast) *in Zion, to give them beauty for ashes, the oil of joy for mourning, the garment of praise for the <u>spirit of heaviness</u>..." Isaiah 61:3 (NKJV)*

The third part of the Scripture speaks of "to let the oppressed go free". I believe that the psalmist was praying against just such a spirit of oppression when he wrote:

"Keep me as the apple of Your eye; hide me under the shadow of Your wings, <u>from the wicked who oppress me</u>, from my deadly enemies who surround me." Psalms 17:8-9 (NKJV)

Lastly, we also have "and that you break every yoke". Sometimes in this world, it may happen that we (or someone that we love) are yoked together with people whom the enemy can use to lead us astray. In those times, it should also be covered with prayer and fasting so that we (or the person that we hold dear) may gain our deliverance.

"Do not be unequally yoked with unbelievers [do not make mismated alliances with them or come under a different yoke with them, inconsistent with your faith]. For what partnership have right living and right standing with God with iniquity and lawlessness? Or how can light have fellowship with darkness? What harmony can there be between Christ and Belial [the devil]? Or what has a believer in common with an unbeliever? What agreement [can there be between] a temple of God and idols? For we are the temple of the living God; even as God said, I will dwell in and with and among them and I will walk in and with and among them, and I will be their God, and they shall be My people. So, come out from among [unbelievers], and separate (sever) yourselves from them, says the Lord..." II Corinthians 6:14-17 (AMPC)

I come from a family where divorce, abortions, illegitimate children, adultery, incest, etc. was rife, so I have much to work through. Sometimes my breakthrough can take months, and in other cases years, but God is always faithful.

In chapter 2 I spoke at length about the heart, how it contains evil and good treasure, and how important your heart is to God. The Bible also has this to say about your heart:

"Only fear the Lord and serve Him faithfully with <u>all</u> your heart..." I Samuel 12:24 (AMPC)

There are many Scriptures in God's Word that tell you to love and serve God with *all* your heart, or with your *whole* heart. I have always thought this to be the easiest Scripture in the Bible to obey. I would read those Scriptures and in my own mind, I would tick that Scripture off as "done".

Do you love and serve God with your whole heart? What does it mean to serve God with your whole heart? Does it mean that you should serve God passionately? What if the Lord meant this Scripture literally? What if He really wants us to serve Him with our whole (meaning, every inch of our) heart?

If that is the case, then I Samuel 12:24 becomes a very complicated Scripture. Especially if you look at Mark 7:21-22:

"For from within, [that is] out of the hearts of men, come base and wicked thoughts, sexual immorality, stealing, murder, adultery, coveting (a greedy desire to have more wealth), dangerous and destructive wickedness, deceit; unrestrained (indecent) conduct; an evil eye (envy), slander (evil speaking, malicious misrepresentation, abusiveness), pride (the sin of an uplifted heart against God and man), foolishness (folly, lack of sense, recklessness, thoughtlessness)." Mark 7:21-22 (AMPC)

If all these evil treasures are contained in, and taking up space in your heart, are you then truly loving and serving God with *all* of your heart? Or are you only serving the Lord with the part of your heart that is left over?

The evil treasures that you store up in your heart unwittingly keeps you from serving God with all your heart. In reality, you are only serving God with the small part of your heart that is not filled with evil. Allow me to explain: The evil in your heart can come in the form of gossip, slander, addictions, strife, etc. If you are gossiping (for example), are you serving God at that moment? If you are slandering someone (another example), are you serving God in that moment? Therefore, you serve God only with the part of your heart that is not given to gossip or slander (or any other sin). And here is the point that I was trying to make in chapter 2: One of the main reasons for fasting is to restore your broken relationship with the Lord by gaining deliverance from the evil treasures in your heart. As you systematically remove the evil treasure from your heart, you begin to serve God with more and more of your heart – not only the small pieces left over after the evil treasure has taken up the most of the space.

<u>**Deliverance from Addictions:**</u>

For many years, I have struggled with addictions. In my bloodline, addiction is very prominent. I had an aunt and a sister who were both alcoholics. Now here is the sneaky truth about addiction:

When you have addiction in your bloodline, it will not always manifest in the same addiction. If, for example, your mother was addicted to drugs and you happen to escape the curse of drug addiction you may think that you do not suffer from addiction like your mother did. However, if you look carefully at your own life, you will find that there are other things that you may have an addiction to e.g. food, sex, television, games, pornography, etc. An addiction is simply to have an inability (or great difficulty) to stop indulging in a substance or an action. This addiction (whatever it may be) will always be on your mind. You will not be able to stop thinking about it. You will always try making plans to indulge in it, and when you try to stop, you may invariably find yourself giving way to it again. In my life, my addiction is television. For years, I have been praying for deliverance, and in the process, the Lord has taught me much about this ugly spirit. After a few years of crying out to the Lord, He showed me that, when you pray for deliverance from an addiction, you should fast from that specific addiction as you pray. The old analogy about starving the dog that you don't want to grow. I must admit that those have been the most difficult fasts that I have ever undertaken. In all honesty, I have failed those fasts on occasion by not being able to complete them, but I have kept on trying.

As I pushed through, the Lord showed me one day that addiction is also an evil treasure of the heart. Remember, the heart is the treasure chest of your being. Everything that appeals to your fleshly nature, is stored up in your heart as evil treasure. There are three main entry points for treasure to enter into your heart:

1. The eyes:

Your eyes are a doorway into your heart. Be selective with what you look at! At some point you looked at something that was appealing to your fleshly nature (the part that is at enmity with God) and your heart took hold of it, and stored it as a treasured item e.g. pornography.

"[That is] because the mind of the flesh [with its carnal thoughts and purposes] is hostile to God, for it does not submit itself to God's Law; indeed it cannot. So then those who are living the life of the flesh [catering to the appetites and impulses of their carnal nature] cannot please or satisfy God, or be acceptable to Him." Romans 8:7-8 (AMPC)

2. The ears:

Your ears are also a doorway into your heart. Be equally selective what you listen to!

"Then He [Jesus] said to them, 'Take heed what you hear.'" Mark 4:24 (NKJV)

3. Your bloodline:

The last doorway is of somewhat of a different nature. This doorway is through inheritance. This is how it works: What is stored up in your heart is referred to by the Bible as "treasure". Here is the issue with treasure: Treasure becomes an inheritance to your children when you die (whether good or evil). Treasure does not disappear when you die - it is carried over to your descendants through inheritance. Every treasure in your heart will be carried over to your children through inheritance – whether good or evil. In fact, in your own heart (whether you want it, or not) will be your own inheritance that you received from your ancestors – whether the inheritance from your ancestors are richly good, or richly evil. The inheritance from your ancestors will inherently be stored in your heart – the place where family treasures are kept.

Is there a door leading from your heart? *The tongue.*

"For out of the abundance of the heart the mouth speaks."
Matthew 12:34 (NKJV)

If you want to know what is in your heart, just listen carefully to what comes out of your mouth. Do you gossip? It flows over from your heart. Do you cuss? It also flows from your heart.

So it is also with addiction. Addiction most certainly comes from your heart. Your heart has stored up addiction as a treasure. You may wonder, then, how addiction is able to manifest in different areas? Here is what the Lord showed me: The *root* of addiction is *idolatry*. When you suffer from addiction it means that you have a root of idolatry in your heart.

Idolatry is simply an extreme admiration or <u>love of something</u>. It is the worship of something as a god, and it will cause you to have an excessive attachment or infatuation with something. Sound familiar? Sounds a lot like an addiction to me.

Addiction is having the penchant for idolizing things in your life. You have a penchant towards developing an infatuation and excessive love for something (not necessarily something good), to the point that it may eventually consume or destroy you. This makes it nearly impossible to stop serving and loving that addiction. It forces you to always place it first – even above God. When addiction is in your heart, that part of your heart can never belong to God and serve Him, because it will be dedicated to serving your addictions.

"<u>No servant is able to serve two masters;</u> for either he will hate the one and love the other, or he will stand by and be devoted to the one and despise the other." Luke 16:13-14 (AMPC)

This is the same with every evil treasure in your heart. Do you struggle with gossip? <u>The love</u> of discussing other people and their business is an evil treasure in your heart.

Do you struggle with unforgiveness? This is simply the <u>love</u> of holding on to hate and the <u>love</u> of revenge. It is an evil treasure in your heart.

Do you struggle with adultery? This is simply the <u>love</u> of attention from others – an evil treasure stored up in your heart.

All of these sins in your heart has one thing in common: <u>*love*</u>. You <u>love</u> the payoff for these sins more than you love God, and therefore you cannot stop – even for Him.

"Jesus answered them, Verily, verily, I say unto you, Whosoever commits sin is the servant of sin." John 8:34 (KJV)

Allow me to recap for you: When something (good or evil) is treasured in your heart, it is because you hold onto it dearly. *You love it.* All of us have many little "sins" that we struggle with every day. All these little foxes that we cannot seem to shake off are sins that we inadvertently hold on to and enjoy committing.

Let us be honest: We cannot shake gossip and slander, because we enjoy it too much. We love hearing and sharing news about others, and we love the importance of sharing something new and juicy that no one else knew about.

"The words of a talebearer are like tasty trifles, and they go down into the inmost body." Proverbs 18:8 (NKJV)

That is the problem with dealing with sin in our lives – we love doing it! Without realizing it we love being proud, because we feel that we deserve to be elevated above others. We want to believe that we are special and different – more so than others. We cannot stop looking at pornography, because we find pleasure in it. We love the feeling and the excitement we get from it. We love being envious of others, because we feel like we are justified. We feel so much more deserving than others. We love to do all these sins (whatever sins you are "struggling" with), because we love the pay-out we get from them. *This is because they are treasures in your heart.*

Here is another truth: You cannot simply stop sinning because you want to live a holy life. The only way that you will be able to stop sinning that sin and live a holy life is if God delivers you from that sin, because your heart will keep convincing you to commit that sin you so love and treasure over and over again. You only *think* you want to stop, but your heart has hidden the fact from you that this sin is treasured within it, thus making you unable to stop. So you will find yourself serving the sin instead of serving God.

Hence therein lies the problem. We begin to pray and fast, asking the Lord to deliver us from that sin – the sin that you secretly love. Listen, God will never deliver you from a something that you love and treasure. Why? Because you are praying with two minds. On the one hand you think you hate the sin, but on the other hand you (unknowingly) love it so much that you cannot stop indulging in it. You, my friend, are praying double-minded prayers.

"But he must ask in faith without doubting, for the one who doubts is like a wave of the sea, blown and tossed around by the wind. <u>For that person must not suppose that he will receive anything from the Lord, since he is a double-minded individual,</u> unstable in all his ways." James 1:6-8 (NET)

This Scripture shows that a double-minded individual is unstable in all his ways, because he has no control over his own life. He is literally like a wave of the sea: "blown and tossed around" by that sin.

Does this mean that it is hopeless to pray and fast for deliverance from these sins? No, never. It simply means that your deliverance may take some time, because now the Lord has to bring you to the point where you no longer love and treasure the sin, but hate the sin so much that you choose (of your own volition) not to engage in it anymore.

I have come to realize that no sin is free of charge. I always tell my husband that sin is like carbs – you will never get away with indulging in it – it has to show somewhere. Every sin will cost you in the end, and it is usually something that you hold very dear in your life. Only when the revelation and realization truly comes of what that sin may cost you in your life, can you begin to hate that sin with your whole heart. You begin to hate the sin when the thing that you stand to lose in your life is more precious to you than the sin. Only God can give you such a revelation and bring you to that place, and it is done after much fasting and prayer. Let me give you an example from my life:

Many years ago, I began to realize that I had a problem with strife. It began to manifest in my life at a time when I became more and more aware of the concept of holiness. For those of you that are not familiar with the term "strife", allow me to explain. Strife is to cause constant conflict. It is like the dripping of a tap. You have to bicker continuously over every little thing. In hindsight I realize now that this was also a generational spirit that came down my bloodline. It was always hidden from me, because everyone in my family suffers from it and we always thought of ourselves as people who stand up for our rights. However, as the Lord willed I married a very sweet, non-confrontational husband. His sweet nature (coupled with much fasting and prayer about holiness) began to make me intensely aware of the evil nature of mine that wanted to constantly have something to say about everything. This became so bad that I realized that if I didn't get my deliverance from that spirit of strife, that I could very well lose my husband. I began to hate that sin in my heart with a great ferocity, and I cried out to God night and day with fasting.

I would pray something like this: *Lord, please deliver me from this spirit of strife. I do not want to lose my husband. I do not want to carry over this evil inheritance to my children. Please don't let them have to deal with this evil in my life that threatens to destroy all that I hold dear. God, this strife is destroying my testimony as a believer. What testimony do I have if I am constantly involved in quarrelling? Please deliver me. I can no longer live with this evil. Either I will break, or it will break – please don't let it be me!*

This went on for some time. I would even get up at night (unable to sleep) and cry out to God continuously. Then, one morning I woke up and the Lord had literally delivered me overnight. I could immediately feel the difference within me, and I could see it in my marriage and in all my relationships. You see, the Lord showed me what I stood to lose if I did not deal with that sin in my life, and what I stood to lose was infinitely more important to me than the sin itself. At that point, my prayers reached a peak, and God graciously stepped in and delivered me. In the years since then I have learned to deeply appreciate peace in my home and in my life. I realize the value of it, and I know what I had to go through to receive that gift. This is merely the first of many such examples in my life where the Lord has shown Himself faithful. To reach the point where you realize the impact of the sin in your life and begin to hate it as you cry out to the Lord for deliverance will not be a comfortable time for you. It is a time of desperation – a tipping point in your life that feels much like a fire, but in the end it yields holy fruit and is truly worth it.

As I draw to the close of my chapter there is one more area I would like to discuss, and it is the area of soul ties. Soul ties is on my list of things that you cannot get deliverance from except by prayer and fasting as is also indicated by this following Scripture:

"Is not this the fast that I have chosen: <u>to loose the bonds of wickedness</u>..." Isaiah 58:6 (NKJV)

Many years ago, the Lord showed me how stubborn soul ties truly were. I had done a prayer previously against soul ties and had thought it to be enough. However, I went through a time where the Lord began to show me how soul ties were negatively affecting my life and my marriage.

"Let us break their bands [of restraint] asunder and cast their cords [of control] from us." Psalm 2:3 (AMPC)

As I began to fast against soul ties, the Holy Spirit began to teach me about the evil bonds that tie us to people and things and are used by the enemy as an open door into our lives. It got to the point where I began to make soul tie lists for each person in my household and myself. I would use these lists as I fasted for deliverance. During this time I realized just how broad soul ties can be. I learned that there were all kinds of soul ties e.g. rape soul ties, incest soul ties, soul ties binding you to ungodly people, soul toes binding you to ungodly sects, sex soul ties, rejection soul ties, trauma soul ties, etc.

As you pray and fast, be aware that God is faithful. You may not receive your deliverance in a short time, but if you persevere, God will set you free indeed. It is possible to get rid of all these things that hinder your walk with God.

CHAPTER 8

FASTING TO SANCTIFY YOURSELF

"Who can understand his errors? Cleanse me from secret faults."
Psalm 19:12 (AMPC)

If I have to think back over all the years of fasting I think one of the most frequently asked questions I have been asked to answer is whether or not a person should abstain from having sex with their spouse whilst fasting.

"Do not deprive one another except with consent for a time, that you may give yourselves to fasting and prayer; and come together again so that Satan does not tempt you because of your lack of self-control." I Corinthians 7:5 (NKJV)

At first, I didn't have an answer. I would simply reply with, *"Sorry, I haven't had a revelation about that yet. Why don't you pray about it?"* It was only after a few years of fasting that the Lord broke through one day and opened up this concept for me.

Now, first off, I just want to clear up the fact that this Scripture refers to a married couple – to a husband and a wife. The Bible is clearly speaking about a husband and a wife when you look at the preceding Scriptures:

"Let the <u>husband</u> render to his <u>wife</u> the affection due her, and likewise also the <u>wife</u> to her <u>husband</u>. The <u>wife</u> does not have authority over her own body, but the <u>husband</u> does. And likewise the <u>husband</u> does not have authority over his own body, but the <u>wife</u> does." I Corinthians 7:3-4 (NKJV)

Thus, when read in context, it is clear that I Corinthians 7:5 refers to a man and a woman in covenant relationship (marriage) with each other.

Now when you take a good look at I Corinthians 7:5 you will see that the husband and wife may abstain from sex in the marriage *only with consent* for a time of fasting and prayer, after which they must be reunited again in intimacy. Why should a husband and wife abstain from sex to fast and pray? Let me take you back to the Old Testament for a moment:

"Then the Lord said to Moses, 'Go to the people and sanctify them today and tomorrow, and make them wash their clothes and be ready for the third day, for on the third day the Lord will come down on Mount Sinai in the sight of all the people'...Then Moses went down from the mountain to the people and sanctified the people, and they washed their clothes. He said to the people, 'Be ready for the third day. Do not go near your wives." Exodus 19:10-11;14-15 (NET)

The Lord was about to make a visitation to Israel, and Israel needed to sanctify themselves accordingly. Sanctify meaning to set themselves apart for the Lord.

Now it may happen that you desire a visitation from the Lord. A visitation in which you wish for the Lord to reveal Himself to you in a personal way. If that is the case, then you need to undertake a sanctification-fast. The goal with this fast is to sanctify yourself and set yourself apart for the Lord alone, so that you may prepare yourself for an intimate meeting with Him. A revelation of Who He is. That would be the goal of a sanctification-fast.

When you undertake a sanctification-fast, the Bible shows us clearly that it should last for a period of three days, and no longer.

"Then the Lord said to Moses, 'Go to the people and sanctify <u>them today and tomorrow</u>, and make them wash their clothes <u>and be ready for the third day, for on the third day the Lord</u> <u>will come down on Mount Sinai in the sight of all the people'</u> Exodus 19:10-11 (NET)

I believe that the period of your sanctification should take no longer than three days.

Firstly, because the Lord felt three days were sufficient for Him. Secondly, because when any fast is undertaken I have found that the enemy sees it as an opportune time to attack. Obviously, he hates a successful fast and all the breakthrough-power released by it. I have found that the enemy may attack in different ways during a fast, but mostly the attacks will be directed at your mind and the people closest to you whose behaviour has an influence over you. Therefore, I feel that the apostle Paul admonishes us to *"not deprive one another except with consent for a time"*, after which we must resume marital relations. This is for our own protection within our marriage. Any longer than the necessary three days and you will leave your marriage open to attacks of temptation from Satan. The Bible is very practical, and therefore makes provision for us to protect our marriage whilst undergoing a sanctification-fast.

Intimacy in a marriage is very important for various reasons, and as a result it needs to be protected. In a marriage the husband, as the God-appointed head of the home, has a great amount of authority when he takes up his position and authority in prayer. There is a specific rank structure when it comes to the Godly family.

"But I want you to know that the head of every man is Christ, the head of woman is man, and the head of Christ is God." I Corinthians 11:3 (NKJV)

And again:

"For the husband is the head of the wife, as also Christ is the head of the church; and He is the Savior of the body." Ephesians 5:23 (NKJV)

Now it is important in a Godly marriage that the wife does not withhold her body from her husband.

"The wife does not have [exclusive] authority over her own body, but the husband [has his rights]" I Corinthians 7:4 (AMPC)

Like I said before, the husband has tremendous God-given authority as the head of the home, and as such, also over the wife's body as this Scripture indicates. The husband may take up his authority and command depression or illness, for example, to leave his wife's body, and it will obey. The husband can speak to his wife's body and command it to come in line with God's Word and be healed, and it must obey. However, when the wife withholds her body from *intimacy* with her husband, then she also withholds her body from her husband's *authority*. This means that the husband does now not have the amount of authority over his wife's body and life in prayer as he ought to, in order to come against the attacks of the enemy. The KJV of the Bible very appropriately puts it this way:

"The wife does not have power of her own body, but the husband" I Corinthians 7:4 (KJV)

Wives, withholding your body from marital relations with your husband literally robs your husband of his authority and spiritual power over you. Authority and power that can be used for your protection and healing. That is why it is so vitally important that you adhere to Paul's admonition when he warns you to only withhold your bodies from each other for a short while (with consent), after which you must come together again. It protects your marriage and your life in so many ways.

The apostle Paul also tells us that we should not withhold our bodies from each other for prayer and fasting *without consent*. It is very important that both parties consent to such a sanctification-fast. If you wish to undertake such a fast, your spouse must consent. You cannot undertake such a fast without your spouses' consent, because it will result in all kinds of negative backlash. Firstly, your spouse may feel rejected if you do not have consent, which may also leave the door open to temptation attacks on your marriage.

Most importantly, your spouse may begin to resent the Lord and your beliefs. If your spouse is either not a born-again believer, or not very strong in the Lord, then that is definitely not the route that you wish to go. Your goal should be to draw your spouse closer to you and to the Lord as a result. If you wish to undertake such a fast and feel that your spouse may not easily agree to it, then you should pray about it at length before you approach your spouse. The Biblical approach is for your spouse to agree and to consent. If you are not married, well then you don't have that obstacle to cross, do you?

So, we have established that the Biblical period of your fast should be three days, and that there should be consent between a husband and a wife before such a fast is undertaken. Let's take a look at the requirements of the sanctification-fast. During a sanctification fast the Lord wishes you to sanctify yourself for Him – *literally to set yourself apart for Him.* God told Moses that the Israelites should wash their clothes:

"Then the Lord said to Moses, 'Go to the people and sanctify them today and tomorrow, and make them wash their clothes" Exodus 19:10 (NET)

We all know that white, clean garments speak of righteousness and purity.

Let your garments be always white [with purity]" Ecclesiastes 9:8 (AMPC)

Whenever white garments are mentioned in the Bible it refers to our righteousness and our purity.

"Wash me thoroughly [and repeatedly] from my iniquity and guilt and cleanse me and make me wholly pure from my sin!" Psalm 51:2

When we do a sanctification fast in preparation for a visitation from the Lord, then it is God's will that we go into a time of repentance before Him – a time spent in deep repentance in His presence.

And there is only one thing that can wash us white as snow: *the precious blood of Jesus.*

"If we [freely] admit that we have sinned and confess our sins, He is faithful and just (true to His own nature and promises) and will forgive our sins [dismiss our lawlessness] and [continuously] cleanse us from all unrighteousness [everything not in conformity to His will in purpose, thought, and action]." I John 1:9 (AMPC)

This is the type of fast in which your main purpose should be to sit in the presence of Jesus continually, with your focus mainly on repentance. You must ask the Lord continuously to search your heart, and as He reveals to you, you must respond with a deep and sincere repentance. It's a fast in which you will lay it all bare to the Lord. The Lord will go deep into your heart and reveal things to you that you never knew was there. I must warn you that it may be a very painful and emotional fast, but when the Lord reveals Himself to you, it will be worth the while ten times over.

Another requirement of this fast is the part where you and your spouse are not to have marital relations. In fact, Moses puts it like this:

"Do not go near your wives." Exodus 19:15 (NET)

Moses is very clear when he instructs the Israelites not to touch their wives. This not only means no marital relations, but it means no touching of any kind and no kissing (which is also touching). You are to abstain from any kind of touching in regards to your spouse. If you are not married, but (hopefully) in a godly relationship, then you are to abstain from any touching in that relationship too. The whole point of this fast is to set yourself apart for the Lord. This is not the type of fast that I would undertake whilst working (speaking now to the working people like me). This is the type of fast that calls for a godly getaway for three days. Three days of solitude in which there is only you and the Lord. No pollutions from the world, and no family and friends distracting you from closeness with the Lord. If you talk to anyone during these three days, let it be only to the Lord. Separate yourself completely to the Lord as you wait on Him to sanctify you, so that He may reveal Himself to you.

CHAPTER 9

FASTING: A FEAST

"You shall rejoice in your Feast, you, your son and daughter, your manservant and maidservant, the Levite, the transient and the stranger, the fatherless, and the widow who are within your towns." Deuteronomy 16:14 (AMPC)

We have spoken at length about fasting and all the different types of fasts that you can partake in, but there is one thing that I felt in my heart that I needed to share with you. It is that fasting is not a sad and somber time. Fasting is, in fact, a time of great excitement. A time that preceeds change and breakthrough. Fasting is most definitely a time of celebration. Alternatively, as the Bible puts it: fasting is a "[spiritual] delight".

If you turn away...from doing your own pleasure on My holy day, and call the Sabbath a [spiritual] delight, the holy day of the Lord honourable, and honor Him and it...then will you delight yourself in the Lord" Isaiah 58:13-14 (AMPC)

Did you know, in Biblical times when a king held a feast, they celebrated by handing out food and wine to the people?

"Then the king gave a great feast for all his princes and his servants, Esther's feast; and he gave a holiday [or a lessening of taxes] to the provinces <u>and gave gifts</u> in keeping with the generosity of the king." Esther 2:18 (AMPC)

This is very much what we discussed in chapter 4 when we spoke about actively fasting. When you actively fast according to Isaiah chapter 58, then you also hand out food and clothes to the needy.

"Is it not to divide your bread with the hungry and bring the homeless poor into your house – when you see the naked, that you cover him, and that you hide not yourself from [the needs of] your own flesh and blood?" Isaiah 58:7 (AMPC)

This is exactly how you should celebrate your fast, by handing out food and clothes to the needy so that they may celebrate the joy of the Lord and the honour of serving Him with you.

"And when these days were completed, the king made a feast for all the people present in Shushan the capitol, both great and small, a seven-day feast in the court of the garden of the king's palace." Esther 1:5 (AMPC)

Here you once again see the king sharing his own feast with his people as he celebrates. Even to this day when you celebrate a birthday, you do so by inviting people over to share in a meal or cake that you have prepared.

Did you know that to the Lord a feast and a fast is synonym? Take a look at some of the different feasts that the Lord instituted:

1. **<u>The Feast of Tabernacles</u>**

In this feast the Israelites fasted from the comfort of their own home and bed to commemorate the fact that the Lord led them out of Egypt and into the wilderness for 40 years.

"Also on the fifteenth day of the seventh month [nearly October], when you have gathered in the fruit of the land, you shall keep the feast of the Lord for seven days, the first day and the eighth day each a Sabbath. And on the first day you shall take the fruit of pleasing trees [and make booths of them], branches of palm trees, and boughs of thick (leafy) trees, and willows of the brook; and you shall rejoice before the Lord your God for seven days. You shall keep it as a feast to the Lord for seven days in the year, a statute forever throughout your generations; you shall keep it in the seventh month. You shall dwell in booths (shelters) for seven days: All native Israelites shall dwell in booths, that your generations may know that I made the Israelites dwell in booths when I brought them out of the land of Egypt." Leviticus 23:39-43 (AMPC)

This Scripture shows how the Lord connects a fast with a feast, and note in verse 40 how the Lord instructs the Israelites to rejoice before Him for seven days as they fast/feast. Rejoice refers to a feeling of delight and the showing of great joy.

2. **The Feast of Trumpets**

During this feast the Israelites fast from doing any work, offer up offerings to the Lord and blow horns as a call to Israel to gather for God's Word of redemption.

"On the first day of the seventh month [on New Year's Day of the civil year], you shall have a holy [summoned] assembly; you shall do no servile work. It is a day of blowing of trumpets for you [everyone blowing who wishes, proclaiming that the glad New Year has come and that the great Day of Atonement and the Feast of Tabernacles are now approaching]." Numbers 29:1 (AMPC)

3. **The Feast of Unleavened Bread (Passover)**

Here the Israelites fast by eating only unleavened bread and by refraining from doing any servile work to commemorate the night before the Israelites left Egypt, when they didn't have enough time to allow for their bread to rise, because of their sudden departure.

"[In celebration of the Passover in future years] seven days shall you eat unleavened bread; even the first day shall you put away leaven [symbolic of corruption] out of your houses; for whoever eats leavened bread from the first day until the seventh day, that person shall be cut off from Israel. On the first day you shall hold a solemn and holy assembly, and on the seventh day there shall be a solemn and holy assembly; no kind of work shall be done in them, save [preparation of] that which every person must eat – that only may be done by you." Exodus 12:15-16 (AMPC)

4. **Purim**

A feast in memory of the extraordinary deliverance of the Jews from the murderous plot of Haman. A day of fasting is kept after which the Jews send gifts to the poor and also exchange gifts with each other. Although this was a fast/feast that was instituted by the Israelites and not the Lord, it is clear that the Israelites had by then also made the connection between a fast and a feast.

"And Mordecai recorded these things, and he sent letter to all the Jews who were in all the provinces of the King Ahasuerus, both near and far, to command them to keep the fourteenth day of the month of Adar and also the fifteenth, yearly, as the days on which the Jews got rest from their enemies, and as the month which was turned for them from sorrow to gladness and from mourning into a holiday – <u>that they should make them days of feasting and gladness, days of sending choice portions to one another and gifts to the poor." Esther 9:20-22</u> (AMPC)

One Hebrew word for festival is "hāg" (from the verb signifying "to dance"), which when applied to religious services, indicated that they were occasions of joy and gladness.

When our fasts become feasts, we celebrate the goodness of the Lord and delight ourselves in the Lord, by sharing our joy with others around us, whether they know Him or not. In every one of these fasts the Israelites celebrated their feasts by singing and rejoicing in the Lord

"And the Israelites who were in Jerusalem kept the Feast of Unleavened Bread for seven days <u>with great joy. The Levites and priests praised the Lord day by day, singing with instruments of much volume to the Lord.</u>" II Chronicles 30:21 *(AMPC)*

CHAPTER 10

ONE FLESH

"And the two shall become one flesh, so that they are no longer two, but one flesh." Mark 10:8 (AMPC)

This may seem like a strange topic to discuss in a fasting book. The concept of a man and a woman becoming one (or "one flesh") when they get married is a well-known concept throughout the Bible.

"But from the beginning of creation God made them male and female. For this reason a man shall leave [behind] his father and his mother and be joined to his wife and cleave closely to her permanently, and the two shall become one flesh, so that they are no longer two, but one flesh. What therefore God has united (joined together), let no man separate or divide." Mark 10:6-9 (AMPC)

This is a very interesting concept to explore. As a man and a woman unite in marriage, they may become intimate. This is a godly union, for God is the One Who instituted the concept of marriage. As they unite in intimacy, they become one flesh. The concept of one flesh is not only in working whilst they are intimate. No, "one flesh" is a permanent spiritual condition, in which the husband and the wife are now united, and function together as one flesh – literally as one spiritual person.

"Even so husbands should love their wives as [being in a sense] their own bodies. He who loves his own wife loves himself. For no man ever hated his own flesh, but nourishes and carefully protects and cherishes it, as Christ does the church" Ephesians 5:28-29 (AMPC)

I have realized that the concept of one flesh is a secret that needs to be explored more deeply. If you look at this Scripture, you will see that when you are one flesh in marriage you should nurture each other and look well after each other as if the other was your own body. My husband and I have completely bought into this concept.

Now there are certain privileges that come with being one flesh. In my own marriage, I have found that my husband and I are so closely connected, that we mostly have the same thoughts even without the other one knowing about it. We are known for completing each other's sentences. I believe it's because we have fully embraced our union of "one flesh" and we abide by the rules of treating the other as if it were yourself. Surely, you will not break down your own body willingly and knowingly? We do not break each other down with our words, and we take care to nourish each other as if we are nourishing our own bodies. However, as nice as it sounds, this is not where the connection ends. Many years ago, after the birth of my second son, I went through a very strenuous period of fasting. I went through an exceptionally difficult time with my baby's health, so I stepped up my fasting routine. For months, I would fast one week on and one week off. I was determined to address my son's ill health and I kept pushing into the Spirit for answers and for healing. As a result my health began to suffer – more specifically, my metabolism slowed down tremendously, and for the first time in my life, I picked up a weight problem. As I realised what was happening in my own body, I began to pray about it. In fact, I cried out to God, asking Him what I should do. The dilemma was that I refused to stop fasting, because I needed that power released into our lives. However, with each fast, my health deteriorated. One night I was once again up during the night praying, crying out to God, and asking Him for a solution to my problem. On this specific night, the Lord came through for me.

The Lord spoke into my spirit and showed me that my husband and I are one flesh. Therefore, if the one fasted, the other had no need to fast as well, but only to pray with, and the same amount of power will be released as if both were fasting. In all honesty, I had difficulty wrapping my mind around this statement of the Lord initially. At first, I tried to implement this, but I had difficulty getting my mind straight. It felt so strange not to be pushing through some kind of suffering, but yet to reap the same results in prayer as my husband fasted for us at times. On some level, I felt that I needed to be the one fasting and suffering; otherwise, it wouldn't yield the same results. However, the Lord quickly spoke to me, and showed me that fasting should not be a legalistic thing. Answers to prayer does not come by how hard we suffer, but in how much faith we use. In the end, I pushed through and became more accustomed to the practice. This helped me tremendously with my health and my fasting routine. My husband and I ended up taking turns to fast. On Tuesdays, I would fast for us, and we would both pray as if we were fasting. On Thursdays, my husband would do the fasting, and again we would pray as if both of us were fasting. So, we learned to operate by faith in God's Word, and not to lean on legalism, and slowly, but surely, my health began to improve.

A few months after that incident the Lord revealed something else to me. I had been praying for the company where my husband worked at the time. The Lord had shown me the strongman over his workplace, and as a result, I was fasting, praying, and doing much warfare in order to take that company back for the Lord. One night I was up praying and doing warfare for my husband's company, when the Lord interjected and clearly gave me a Scripture:

"Every place that the sole of your foot will tread upon I have given you" Joshua 1:3 (NKJV)

I sat in silence for a moment, puzzled. After a few seconds, I spoke to the Lord and said, *'Lord, but I have never been to his company before? My feet have not tread there.'* After which the Lord immediately answered, *'No, but your husband has, and you are one flesh, aren't you?'* Immediately a light went on for me and I understood exactly where the Lord was taking me. He was showing me that I could claim that company back for the Lord, whilst standing on Joshua 1:3 on the basis that my husband (whose feet had treaded there) and I were one flesh.

A small concept like being one flesh can open up so many possibilities for us, provided we are able to implement these revelations in faith.

CHAPTER 11

FASTING REWARDS

"I am coming quickly; hold fast what you have, so that no one may rob you and deprive you of your crown." Revelation 3:11 (AMPC)

Do we as believers receive rewards from the Lord? Do all people receive rewards from the Lord, or only believers? Should we purposely work for and gather heavenly rewards? These are only a few of the questions that people have when the topic of heavenly rewards come into discussion. Hopefully these questions may be answered for you in this chapter.

It is important that you understand that rewards can only be earned whilst you are on earth. When you get to heaven, all the rewards that were not issued on earth will be issued to you in heaven, but you can no longer work for rewards once you are in heaven.

"Do not gather and heap up and store up for yourselves treasures on earth, where moth and rust and worm consume and destroy, and where thieves break through and steal. But gather and heap up and store for yourselves treasures in heaven, where neither moth nor rust nor worm consume and destroy, and where thieves do not break through and steal" Matthew 6:19-20 (AMPC)

Firstly, I want to focus your attention on the fact that there are two dimensions at play in this Scripture. In fact, they are not only mentioned, but they are pitted against each other. You can see the word "earth" which refers to the first dimension, better known to us as "the world". Then you have the word "heaven" in the second verse, which is the second dimension, better known to us as "God's kingdom".

Now when you are born again and a child of God, you should naturally focus on the second dimension of God's kingdom, because that is now where you belong, and that is where you will be spending eternity. In essence, this Scripture tells you not to lay up treasures in this world, because this world is fleeting - it will pass away and then you will have nothing left of that which you stored up. Treasures stored up in this world have no currency in God's kingdom (heaven), and are of no worth there, which is, of course, our final destination. This Scripture then instructs us (hope you didn't miss the fact that Jesus is instructing us here) to lay up treasures for ourselves in God's kingdom, which is eternal and will never pass away or come to an end. When it comes to rewards (or treasure as the Scripture puts it), it is important to make a decision in which dimension you wish to lay up your treasure. You may be rich in treasure in the world, and reach heaven a pauper, because you stored up your treasure in the wrong bank account. Alternatively, you can be poor in this world, but reach heaven as a wealthy person, because you placed your treasures in the eternal bank account - the one that counts.

Here is the catch, and the important principle to remember: WHEN YOU WORK FOR TREASURE, YOU HAVE TO DECIDE WHERE IT MUST BE STORED. A treasure can only be stored in one place, and your actions and motives decide where that will be. Let me make it clearer to you. Take a look at this Scripture:

"Take heed that you do not do your charitable deeds before men, to be seen by them. Otherwise you have no reward from your Father in heaven. Therefore, when you do a charitable deed, do not sound a trumpet before you as the hypocrites do in the synagogues and in the streets, <u>that they may have glory from men</u>. Assuredly, I say to you, <u>they have their reward</u>. But when you do a charitable deed, do not let your left hand know what your right hand is doing, that your charitable deed may be in secret; and <u>your Father Who sees in secret will Himself reward you openly</u>. Also when you pray, you must not be like the hypocrites, for they love to pray standing in the synagogues and on the corners of the streets, <u>that they may be seen by people</u>. Truly I tell you, <u>they have their reward in full already</u>. But when you pray, go into your [most] private room, and, closing the door, pray to your Father, Who is in secret; <u>and your Father, Who sees in secret; will reward you in the open</u>. ...And when you are fasting, do not look gloomy and sour and dreary like the hypocrites, for they put on a dismal countenance, <u>that their fasting may be apparent to and seen by men</u>. Truly I say to you, <u>they have their reward in full already</u>. But when you fast perfume your head and wash your face, so that your fasting may not be noticed by men but by your Father, Who sees in secret; <u>and your Father, Who sees in secret, will reward you in open</u>."
Matthew 6:1-6;16-18 (NKJV)

In this Scripture where Jesus speaks about rewards the world is again pitted against the kingdom of God. If you do something on this earth, and you do it to be seen, or for popularity, or to make yourself look good or more holy, your reward is automatically stored up in your worldly bank account. Here is the key to storing up treasure for yourself in your heavenly bank account: YOU MUST DENY YOURSELF/YOUR FLESH. You must deny yourself the pleasure of human approval, favour, and glory.

Only then will you have treasure in heaven. Receiving favour, approval and glory from the world will cause your treasure to go straight to your worldly bank account.

"If anyone desires to come after Me, <u>let him deny himself,</u> and take up his cross, and follow Me. For whoever desires to save his life will lose it, but whoever loses his life for My sake will find it. For what profit is it to a man if he gains the whole world, and loses his own soul?" Matthew 16:24-26 (NKJV)

Look at the word that Jesus uses in this Scripture. He speaks about "profit". This Scripture refers to rewards. You must learn to deny yourself the desire and inclination to seek the approval and favour of the people of this world. When you do, and you focus instead on the Lord, your motives and actions become pure and your treasures are stored up in your heavenly bank account. There are rewards for us, and we must be like wise investment bankers - knowing exactly where to store up our treasure so that we can get the most out of it when one day we retire from this life. As Jesus says in this Scripture, you must deny yourself the pleasure of showing off how much you give, or how hard you fast. You must deny yourself the pleasure of trying to prove to others how holy you are, how righteous you are, and how you are always trying to help others. Each time that you do, each time that you do it secretly for only the Lord to see, each time that you do it quietly to seek only God's approval - each time that you deny yourself the worldly pleasure of people's approval - you will lay up for yourself treasure in your heavenly bank account. What profit will it be to you if you gain the whole world's approval and adoration, but miss God's? The reward of people's approval and adoration is not worth much, because people are fickle. Today you have their approval, and tomorrow you are old news and no longer carry their favour. With God, it is different. He is always the same. His measure of approval and favour are always the same. He is not human - not like this one minute, and like that another.

He always judges fairly, and perfectly, giving you what you truly deserve.

Each time you choose God's kingdom over worldly pleasure, and deny yourself, you lay up treasures in heaven. Each time you choose God's kingdom over man's approval and favour, and deny yourself, you lay up treasures in heaven. This also applies to your choice of daily activities. Each time you know that it is time to read your Bible and pray, and you deny yourself the pleasure (for example) of watching that movie on television in order to seek God more, you have treasure in heaven. This world is full of choices. Choose wisely. Choose that which is eternal and carries eternal reward over that which is fleeting and carries a fleeting reward. The fleeting reward of watching a good movie will pass, but the reward of denying yourself that movie to seek God more is eternal. Please note that this is merely an example. I am not saying that you can never watch a movie. Here is the point I am trying to make: When you know there is something you need to do in God's kingdom (whether it is having your daily quiet time, or doing a Bible study, or writing a book), and you deny yourself the pleasure of indulging in worldly activities in order to do what you need to do for the Lord, you will have a heavenly reward.

The important thing to remember is this: Wherever you are storing up your treasures – whether it be in the world, or in heaven – there your treasures will begin to accumulate. When your treasures begin to accumulate in heaven your heart will be with the Lord and with His kingdom, because:

"where your treasure is, there will your heart be also." Matthew 6:21 (AMPC)

Taking rewards back to fasting, let's take a look at all the different rewards that we can get *when we fast in an a way that is acceptable to the Lord*:

1. *"Then shall your light break forth like the morning" Isaiah 58:8 (AMPC)*

"then shall your light rise in darkness" Isaiah 58:10 (AMPC)
As a believer, your goal is to let your light shine in this world. When you fast in a way that is acceptable to the Lord, your light shall become brighter and brighter and begin to shine forth from the darkness in this world, as the morning sun breaks forth from darkness at sunrise. The morning light is such a beautiful thing: It breaks the darkness open and then slowly, but surely, it shines brighter and brighter, lighting up everything that was hidden in the dark, making it manifest in the light.

2. *"And the Lord shall...make strong your bones" Isaiah 58:11 (AMPC)*

"your healing (your restoration and the power of a new life) shall spring forth speedily" Isaiah 58:8 (AMPC)
Do you live in perfect health? God will heal and restore you speedily and make strong your bones.

3. *"your righteousness (your rightness, your justice, and your right relationship with God) shall go before you [conducting you to peace and prosperity], and the glory of the Lord shall be your rear guard." Isaiah 58:8 (AMPC)*

Years ago, whilst fasting one day, I found myself pondering this Scripture. I was somewhere in between a conversation with myself and the Lord, and I was wondering what it meant that our righteousness will go before us. Suddenly the Lord spoke up and asked me a question. He said, *"As a born-again believer, what is your righteousness?"* I thought about it for a while and then I answered, *"The blood of Jesus?"* Immediately the Lord said, *"Yes, the blood of Jesus will go before you, and the glory of the Lord will be your rear guard."* I realized that this spoke of protection on a different level. That type of protection is yours when you fast in a way that is acceptable to the Lord.

4. *"your obscurity and gloom become like the noonday" Isaiah 58:10 (AMPC)*

"and I will make you to ride on the high places of the earth"
Isaiah 58:14 (AMPC)

These two Scriptures speak of promotion. Obscurity refers to the state of being unknown, and unimportant. Though you may have been fasting and serving the Lord in secret, there will come a time when the Lord will promote you and make known to others the value that you have for Him.

"For not from the east nor from the west nor from the south come promotion and lifting up. But God is the judge! He puts down one and lifts up another." Psalm 75:6-7 (AMPC)

5. *Then you shall call, and the Lord will answer; you shall cry, and He will say, Here I am." Isaiah 58:9 (AMPC)*

When you fast as God wants you to, He will hear your cries, and He will answer and say, *"Here I am."*

6. *"And the Lord shall guide you continually" Isaiah 58:11 (AMPC)*

As a believer on a specific God-given path, you need guidance. You are called upon to make many decisions every day. God will reward you by guiding you to make the right decisions and thereby stay on the path that He has for you – the path of provision and protection.

7. *"And the Lord shall... satisfy you in drought and in dry places" Isaiah 58:11 (AMPC)*

This speaks of physical and spiritual provision.

8. *"And you shall be like a watered garden and like a spring of water whose waters fail not." Isaiah 58:11 (AMPC)*

God will refresh you and in turn make you a refreshing, spiritual blessing to those around you. You will be so filled with the Spirit and the power of God that rivers of living waters will flow from your belly to those around you.

"He who believes in Me [who cleaves to and trusts in and relies on Me] as the Scripture has said, From his innermost being shall flow [continuously] springs and rivers of living water." John 7:38 (AMPC)

9. *"And your ancient ruins shall be rebuilt" Isaiah 58:12 (AMPC)*

The Lord will deliver you from the things in your bloodline that hold you back, and restore to you that which was broken down by the enemy – that which currently may lie in ruins. The Lord will restore to you that which He has called you to be from ancient times.

10. *"you shall raise up the foundations of [buildings that have laid waste for] many generations" Isaiah 58:12 (AMPC)*

The Lord will rebuild and restore your spiritual foundation.

11. *"you shall be called Repairer of the Breach. Restorer of streets to Dwell In." Isaiah 58:12 (AMPC)*

The Lord will give you a new name: Repairer of the Breach" and "Restorer of Streets to Dwell In", because you have removed the breach between you and Him as you have prayed and fasted.

12. *"then you will delight yourself in the Lord" Isaiah 58:14 (AMPC)*

Fasting and prayer, when it is done as the Lord requires from us, has the power to transform your mind. Fasting will become a labour of love, and you will delight yourself in the Lord.

13. *"and I will feed you with the heritage [promised for you] of Jacob your father; for the mouth of the Lord has spoken it." Isaiah 58:14 (AMPC)*

The Lord will bring you to the blessing promised to Abraham, Isaac and Jacob.

14. *"[Rather] is not this the fast that I have chosen: to loose the bonds of wickedness, to undo the bands of the yoke, to let the oppressed go free, and that you break every [enslaving] yoke?" Isaiah 58:6 (AMPC)*

As discussed in chapter 7, your fast will generate the type of spiritual power that breaks bondages e.g. chains, addictions, soul ties, oppression, yokes, etc.
All these wonderful rewards are waiting for you when you fast, *provided that you fast as pleases God.*

I pray that this book will be the beginning of great breakthroughs for you. May the Lord confirm every fact in this book to you, and may you implement them and make them yours as you go from strength to strength and from glory to glory, in Jesus' name.

<u>ABOUT THE AUTHOR</u>

Lisa van Vuuren is the founder and overseer of Daniel Ministries. Daniel Ministries is committed to restoring the family as the building blocks of society through foundational deliverance as well as prayer and fasting. Lisa has successfully led a fasting group for children every Tuesday, and a fasting group for marriages every Thursday since 2012, and continues to do so under the guidance of the Lord. Lisa holds a BA degree in Psychology from the University of South Africa. Lisa is a wife to her husband, Ruan, and a mother to her two sons, and they make their home in Kempton Park, South Africa. Find Lisa on www.danielministries.co.za or e-mail her at danielministries500@gmail.com

<u>OTHER BOOKS BY LISA VAN VUUREN</u>

COVENANTING WITH GOD

THE LORD'S SUPPER

RELEASING THE POWER OF GOD OVER YOUR MARRIAGE

RELEASING THE POWER OF GOD OVER YOUR CHILD

RELEASING THE POWER OF GOD OVER YOUR CITY

<u>AFRIKAANS</u>

ONTGIN DIE KRAG VAN GOD OOR JOU KIND

Ingram Content Group UK Ltd
Milton Keynes UK
UKHW021834130323
418508UK00014B/1377